'The fin... I've ever ....d.'
Graham Taylor, former England manager

'The Tommy Cooper comedy award goes to Fred Eyre.'
Daily Telegraph

'The funniest soc... ...ry ever.'
The People

'The hilarious revelations of a wonderful lad who was
laughed at by fate and who laughed right-back'.
Maurice Burton, *Lincolnshire Echo*

'Fred Eyre could have won more caps for England than
Bobby Moore, if only he had been a better player.'
John Charles, Leeds United, Juventus and Wales

'Soccer's favourite wit.'
Daily Mail

'If that ball comes in my garden again you're not getting it back.'
Mrs Jackman, 26 Clough Top Road, Blackley, Manchester 9
1948, 49, 50, 51, 52, 53, 54, 55

'Compulsive reading, it proves a real eye-opener. Highly
recommended and a must for every soccer fan.'
Daily Express

'Fred Eyre's book is a gem. Quite simply *Kicked Into Touch* is the
best and most revealing book about football I've ever read.'
The Observer

'He has turned the lowlights of his career into an art form.'
Robert Philip, *Daily Telegraph*

'One of the funniest and most interesting men in football.
Fred Eyre is a living legend.'
Tony Pritchett, *Sheffield Star*

'Dear Sir,
I have to inform you that you have been granted a free
transfer on the expiry of your present contract.'
W. Griffiths, Secretary, Manchester City FC Ltd

'You are the Vinnie Jones of radio.'
Roy Hudd, broadcaster

'There is only one word to describe that man — legend.'
Neil 'Razor' Ruddock with Mike Read, discussing *Kicked Into Touch*
whiling away the hours in the *I'm A Celebrity Get Me Out Of Here!*
jungle, 2003

kicked into touch
plus extra-time

My mother and father, everything was for them.
Thank you to Judith, who inherited the debris and helped me to
pick up the pieces. My love to Suzanne, Steven,
Claire, Lucy and Emily; everything is for you.
My thanks to Lynn and Mary for their efforts with
the computer and to Mark for his expertise.

Kicked into Touch

PLUS EXTRA-TIME

FRED EYRE

MAINSTREAM
PUBLISHING

EDINBURGH AND LONDON

Reprinted 2007

Published in Great Britain in 2006 by
MAINSTREAM PUBLISHING COMPANY
(EDINBURGH) LTD
7 Albany Street
Edinburgh EH1 3UG

First published by Senior Publications 1981
Second impression published by Pomona 2005
Mainstream edition 2006

ISBN 9781845961473

Every effort has been made to trace all copyright holders.
The publishers will be glad to make good any
omissions brought to their attention

A catalogue record for this book is available
from the British Library

Typeset in Granjon
Typeset by Christian Brett

Printed in Great Britain by
Cox & Wyman Ltd

CONTENTS

HALF-TIME
(THE WORLD IS MY LOBSTER)

EXTRA-TIME

Foreword

by Mark Hodkinson

(*The Times*/Pomona Books)

FOOTBALL HAS HAD TOO MANY BOOKS DEVOTED TO IT. FAR TOO many. The quality-control department has left the building and anyone with a half-decent memory of a half-remembered match is out there publishing his memoirs. The scraps, the scrapes, the sessions – oh, what fun we had. Except we didn't have much fun, did we? Most of them are poor. They each tell the same story in different club colours. They are motivated by unashamed self-indulgence, score settling, or as an adjunct to a player's corporate branding and financial expansionist policy (or, as most of us know it: greed).

It hasn't always been this way. There were once pioneering books written by people with something to say in their own distinctive voice; books driven by nothing more than enthusiasm and a love of the game, however it had treated them, whether they be players or passionate observers. Arthur Hopcraft, Hunter Davies, Barry Hines, Eamon Dunphy, Fred Eyre – these were the founding fathers of modern football literature, the men who got there first, told it like it was and left the rest to scramble among the clichés and rake up the old stories. Of these, Fred Eyre is perhaps the least well known, certainly in literary circles.

The punters certainly know him, and people within the

sport, because since it was first published in 1981 *Kicked Into Touch* has sold in excess of a million copies. I first read the book as a young teenager. I didn't know then to deconstruct, so I took it for what it was: a breezy, funny read about a footballing loser who became a winner. Now I'm all grown-up, I see much more in it. At its heart it has the two most important qualities of any book: it is truthful and it inspires.

Unlike many who write about football, his love of the game is absolute. He makes you want to hunt out your kit again or get along to the next match, whoever is playing. He manages this while still relating the cruelty and injustice of the sport, never resorting to overstatement or self-pity. When, as a boy, he is unexpectedly left out of the team as it is about to play on a Football League ground, you are with him, feeling that awful, heart-drowning pain all over again. And you are with him afterwards when the two men in charge of the team give him neither explanation nor even acknowledgement. You're on your own, kid. We all are.

Fred is not a Dostoevsky or a Hemingway. He is no literary fancy-dan, someone who will attempt a speculative bicycle kick when a neat six-yard pass of a sentence is more effective. He has that great underrated skill of being able to write as he speaks. Turn a few pages and he's with you in the room, talking to you in that voice which is knowing and pragmatic, a quip never more than a few minutes away.

He began his football career in the late 1950s and provides an absorbing snapshot of times past. His world either side of the next match was one of afternoon table-tennis sessions at the YMCA and games of Monopoly in the evenings. He spent his summer holidays at places like Butlins in Pwllheli. In one particular close season we find him, though newly signed to one of the country's most famous football clubs, working as a gardener for the council. It is easy to understand why, back then, footballers and supporters had a strong affinity and how the true spirit of a club was formed. They were all in it together, first among equals.

Football clubs are often portrayed as slick, ultra-professional concerns where every last detail is covered meticulously. This is a myth. Throughout the book, beginning to end, Fred tells us of the game's crude and chaotic nature. We discover managers in charge of more than one club at the same time; a dog (yes, a dog) taking part in team selection; players finding out who their next manager is via the radio as they travel to an away match; a star striker signing for a club thousands of miles away without his current club's knowledge; and managers who can't remember the name of the player they've just signed. Your beloved football club may well be run in this slapdash, hit-and-hope fashion.

He also takes us on a journey to the heart of its people. They're all here: the moaners, the selfish, the stupid, the jokers, the sycophants, the hangers-on, the skivers, the good souls too. All manner of life is pressed together – in the dressing-room, on the team coach, in the shadows after training on a Tuesday evening. And each with their own agenda. Who's in the team? Who's left out? How many more defeats can the manager survive? How much are you earning? Got your next move sorted out? Did you hear the fans moaning out there?

It's a hard game, and Fred never forgets this. The next tackle might be the last. The book opens with a scene routine to football as he receives his own critical injury. Many more follow. Hardly a single character is introduced without exiting stage left on a stretcher and a later reference to a dodgy or sore knee, ankle, shoulder or some other part of his body that will ache or flare up for the rest of his life. If football doesn't fracture a man's dignity, it will find something else to break.

Of course, Fred Eyre is not all grit and toil, far from it. He is known predominantly for making readers laugh. The colour of the kits he has worn has changed down the years but the humour has remained black. And corny too. I laughed when I first read *Kicked Into Touch* and I have laughed again, even though I knew when the punchlines were coming. This doesn't seem to matter. It is a joy to behold a craftsman at work, the arranged marriage between a story and a joke.

The style is perhaps a little quaint now, all these years on, but it must be remembered that Fred (more or less) invented the genre.

When I was a boy, the chapters about his activities outside football held little interest for me. No surprise really, for what is a man's slow rise in the stationery business against the heroism of a life in and around professional football? Reading it again, I see that this is where the real inspiration lies. Unlike football talent, which is God-given, success in real life, both financial and personal, depends on attributes largely within our reach, should we apply them: graft, ingenuity, determination and self-belief.

Unwittingly then, *Kicked Into Touch* is a self-help book. If you want to be successful in business, do what Fred did, or its equivalent: make forty journeys up four flights of stairs carrying reams of paper with a dislocated shoulder. If you want to meet the likes of Frank Sinatra or Ferenc Puskas or Jane Seymour, think on your feet, ask, make it happen. If you are left out of the team at a five-a-side tournament, make up your own team, win the trophy.

His book has endured (40 reprints, no less) because of this indomitable spirit which it captures. Fred Eyre runs at life, makes the world come to him. While doing so he has maintained his morals, done things the right way. When, for example, he leaves the employ of Mr Muir to set up his first shop, he promises not to poach any of his customers. He doesn't really need to say this because we are privy to his resolute decency from the first page onwards.

When I set up Pomona Books (www.pomonauk.co.uk) three years ago, *Kicked Into Touch* was one of the must-have books I wanted to publish. Since first reading it many years earlier I had remained evangelical about it and a little peeved that it had never received the acclaim it deserved. It is difficult now to appreciate how unique it was at the time of first publication and how word spread so defiantly among genuine football fans. It tells its story simply and effectively, in the shop-floor language true to the game.

Thankfully, it once more went down extremely well with the critics. It received unqualified praise from quarters I feared might be a little jaded or sniffy about another book on the life of a football journeyman. No worries. *FourFourTwo* gave it the maximum five stars; *The Guardian* considered it 'a real pleasure' and *When Saturday Comes* acclaimed its 'sardonic wit'. The book, like Fred himself, is still popular among football people too. The launch party held at the City of Manchester Stadium was a resounding success. I opened the door to the venue apprehensively, expecting – I'm ashamed to admit it now – 20 or 30 people. Again, no worries. The room was packed with literally hundreds of football legends and the love (no other word will suffice) that flowed Fred's way was tangible.

Unfortunately, Pomona, as a wholly independent publisher, doesn't quite have the capacity to bring the book to its rightful larger audience, so I have happily granted it a transfer to Mainstream Publishing, on a kind of Bosman. Mainstream has the manpower and wherewithal to give the book a better chance of reaching the Football Everyman, from Plymouth to Aberdeen.

This version is identical to the Pomona one, which was itself a complete revision of the original. Fred updated and extended it considerably. The new chapters, specifically about his time at Sheffield United, prove that the game has changed much less than the marketing folk would have us believe. In short, the slog continues, as do the calamities.

While I worked alongside Fred, many people asked what he was like. Well, he's like this: he takes the manuscript on holiday to Spain with him and texts you corrections and complaints; he phones you on Sunday night at home worried about the syntax of a single sentence; he turns up for every meeting 15 minutes early; he talks to everyone he meets; he ropes his wife, Judith, into every decision, playfully and tenderly; he honours public-speaking engagements knowing 'no one will be there' because he respects the organisers or thinks they're 'good' people; he stocks the shelves at the greetings-card shop he owns in Manchester. There's more: he doesn't drink tea or beer, he exercises regularly and he is one of the happiest and most confident men I have met. In short, his karma is incandescent, though he would never use a word like 'karma'. Or 'incandescent'.

Only once does he hint at another side. I phone him on his mobile one afternoon. He tells me he's 'with his dad'. He explains that he's at the cemetery 'having a quiet moment' at his father's graveside.

'You don't really know this side of me, do you?' he asks.

He's soon talking about City and what he'd like on the book cover and asking me what chapter I'm reading at the moment and did I ring that bloke whose number he gave me last week. Back to being Fred, then. I don't say anything, but I think we do know the other side of him. It's all here.

ONE

The End, or, as it turned out, The Beginning

MANCHESTER CITY 'A' TEAM VERSUS BURY 'A'. NOT really a fixture to remember, you'd think. Another game similar to hundreds of others I'd played in before. How wrong I was—it was to be a very significant day for me.

The routine had been the same that Saturday as it had always been: up about 9 am, just a cup of coffee for my breakfast, then a five-minute walk along Charlestown Road to get the boiled ham for our Sunday tea the next day. I always did this for my mother on Saturdays. You had to be there early to get the best of the ham. She did the main shopping herself later.

The neighbours would call across as I strolled through our council estate:

"Are you playing today, son? Good luck," or just simply, "All the best today."

I was the local boy on his way to the top. I was surrounded by people who wanted me to succeed; good people, Blackley people, and for me there was nowhere like Clough Top Road, where I lived. I loved Clough Top Road and most of the people in it.

We lived in a cul-de-sac off a big street. It had four houses on each side, all joined together, which opened out on to one of Manchester's biggest parks, Boggart Hole Clough. I lived there with my mam and dad and it was a measure of how close-knit we all were that I always called the neighbours on our side Auntie this and Uncle that instead of the usual Mister and Missus.

Blackley was a sprawling council estate in north Manchester where families had gone to live before and after the Second World War. They were honest, decent people, the only type of people I knew. I had trampled through their gardens so many times that my ginger hair passing their windows to retrieve my ball, when it hadn't done what my feet wanted it to, had become a way of life to them, as it was for me.

The 'ham mission' accomplished successfully, I'd nip next door-but-one to Collinge's, the local newsagents, for my supply of Beech Nut chewing gum. No other brand would do. Before my first game for the school team many years before, somebody had slipped me a piece and I played well. A packet of Beech Nut was an essential part of my equipment from then on. Indeed there were occasions when the supply ran out and I had to scour the neighbourhood for an alternative supplier of the stuff. One time I simply couldn't get any and settled for the more expensive Wrigley's. I had an awful game that afternoon and was convinced that the Wrigley's was to blame.

I was in luck that day and with the magic gum safely in my pocket I was soon on my way back home. My routine with the gum was to pop a piece into my mouth just as we kicked off and keep it until I gave a bad pass, then I would spit it out. I abandoned this habit because by the end of the game the taste had gone. If only this were true.

Back home, I packed my gear, had my usual piece of toast and cup of coffee, and was ready to go. My carriage was waiting—in its terminus, the number 88 bus from St John Boscoe's. The usual 'thumbs up' sign from my mother at the door as I left, and I was away. I had to make a quick change in Newton Street, off one bus and onto the number 76, to complete my journey to Maine Road.

I knew the bus timetables better than I knew my two times tables. I had been crossing Manchester this way every day since the age of 11 when I passed my 11-plus to Ducie Avenue School, a mere corner kick away from Maine Road, so the big city held no fears for me.

It was midday and as usual on the day of the big match, even at this relatively early hour there was a buzz about the place that would make the hairs stand up on the back of my neck—I just couldn't wait for it to be my turn. But for today I was still an 'A' team lad battling for stardom and I boarded our Finglands coach for the short journey to Urmston, City's training ground in Chassen Road, with the rest of the boys for the encounter with Bury.

On the coach journey, after a few laughs and jokes with my team-mates, I settled down on the front seat with a young boy aged about seven or eight to keep him company. He was a polite lad, very well mannered, and looked well scrubbed with his tanned cheeks glowing. He was very smart in his school blazer with matching school cap and grey short pants. I liked him and used to enjoy our little chats about football whenever he accompanied the team.

Twenty years later, whenever I saw him I still enjoyed our little chats about football but by then he could speak with a little more authority, having been transferred to Leeds United for a record £350,000 transfer fee from Blackpool, and Paul Hart became one of the best centre-halves in England. He eventually went on to play more than 500 games before becoming a successful youth-team coach at Leeds United and manager at Chesterfield, Nottingham Forest and Barnsley. He was obviously a good listener.

His dad, Johnny, was one of my heroes. When I was a young boy I used to cheer him on from my position behind the goal at the scoreboard end and I admired his goalscoring ability and his bravery. Now he was a team-mate of mine. He was almost at the end of his career and his job was to help us youngsters along.

Just before we reached the ground we always stopped the coach at a local café, The Hughenden, to pick up the cakes and pies for both teams to devour at the end of the game. It was young Paul's job to nip off the coach and bring the pies back quickly while the coach held up all the traffic on Flixton Road.

Finally we were there and the coach drew up at the familiar dirt track leading to the ground. It was neatly kept, with floodlights, and the pitch was usually in good nick. The sun was shining, there was a spring nip in the air and all seemed to be going to plan as I grabbed my favourite peg to change before anybody else claimed it and upset my routine; no problems so far.

Soon we were all changed and ready for action. The team talk took its usual course — Johnny mumbling a few instructions, Dick Niellson banging his right fist into his left palm to indicate that he expected us to give them a bit of stick. An ex-City player, Dick was a tough defender, but as a coach he was kind and patient. He was like a father to me. No wonder, I'd been stuck in his team for so long that I'd known him for almost as long as my father.

"Be positive for the crosses," he'd tell the keeper.

"Mark them tight," were the instructions to the full-backs, and so on through the entire team. But never anything to me. He used to just toss me the ball before I led out the team, with the instructions, "Keep 'em going."

I used to take his lack of communication as a compliment, vainly and stupidly thinking I must be doing everything correctly, that I had nothing else to learn because they had nothing else to tell me and it was just a matter of time before I made the first team.

City at that time were rich in talent for wing-halves, which was my position, but I cared little for their reputations because I thought I was making progress. Slow progress, but progress nevertheless.

Ken Barnes had been a great player. 'The best uncapped wing-half in the country' was the title bestowed on him by sports writers. It was not a title I would have liked. The best capped wing-half would have suited me better. Ken had been a City regular for years, since joining the club from non-league Stafford Rangers, and was a vital member of the team that reached Wembley in two consecutive years. He and Don Revie were the key figures in the famous 'Revie Plan' which revolutionised soccer during the 1950s. But Ken had come to the end of his illustrious career and had joined Wrexham, so that would make more room for me.

His replacement, Bobby Kennedy, a record £45,000 signing from Kilmarnock, was having trouble finding his form and was being switched to full-back in an attempt to help him settle down to life in the English First Division. Alan Oakes, a fine young player, was making the other wing-half spot his own with some sterling performances and his consistency was to later give him a club record of appearances. Former Manchester Schoolboys stars Dave Shawcross and Roy Cheetham were challenging each other for the other wing-half spot, but they were recovering from serious injury and illness respectively so they also had their problems. There was my team-mate, Graham Chadwick, who although we were in the same team, was a couple of years older than me. Then there was a young whippersnapper called Mike Doyle who was coming along on the blind side. He had already caused me a minor problem on his first day at the club by getting involved in a scrap with winger Bobby McAlinden which resulted in me, as a senior player, being called before the manager to receive a good dressing down for 'allowing it to happen'. The two culprits got off scot free.

Finally, John Benson. Four years before, on my first appearance for City, I was obviously nervous but I was put at ease and helped through the game by the inside-forward playing in front of me.

This was John Benson, a stocky kid a couple of years older than me, who although he seemed to be struggling a bit himself (at his age he should have been playing higher than the fifth team), still took time to help me. I've never forgotten this and have liked him ever since. A couple of seasons later, however, he proved to be a big headache as he was switched from a struggling inside-forward to a fine wing-half to provide even more competition for these precious places.

I was far from happy about his switch, but was too frightened of the manager to ask him what it was all about. My opportunity to investigate the situation presented itself as I boarded the number 60 bus outside Baxendale's to go home one day after training. There was only one seat available on the bus and I grabbed it. I needed a seat to rest my legs after a rigorous day's training, and I was surprised to see the other occupant of the seat was Harry Godwin, the scout who had signed me for the club. Here was my chance to discuss the problem of John Benson.

"We've decided he won't make it as an inside-forward so we are just trying him in another position for his swansong," were Harry's exact words. It sounded promising. Twenty years later Benson was still at the club as assistant manager. Some swansong.

Good luck to him. Anyone that helps me, I'm glad when they do well. So while these lads had problems of their own to solve, I would step in, claim my place in the first team and go on to gain a record number of caps for England. Such thoughts were going to change rapidly in the next 65 minutes.

"All the best, lads," I shouted over my shoulder to the crocodile of sky-blue shirts filing out of the dressing-room door behind me.

"Yeah, all the best, Fred," three or four shouted back and we were off, out of the door, studs clinking on the concrete, still one of my favourite sounds even to this day, especially if my feet are inside them, to be met by a roar of indifference from our handful of loyal supporters. Local Urmston pensioners most of them, who loved their football but preferred the simple pleasures of Urmston to the hurly-burly of First Division grounds, with the added bonus of saying to their mates in the pub over a Guinness whenever one of us hit the big time:

"I saw him when he was a kid of 16 in the 'A' team. Knew he was a good 'un the first time I set eyes on him."

In view of the clement weather, the crowd was touching 30 that day. Not thousand, just about 30. I'm not sure exactly because one of them moved while I was counting. Before I could do a recount the whistle had blown to start the game.

It was the usual Bury type of game, hard and dour. It's strange how they used to follow the same pattern against Bury, though usually we managed to win in the end.

Just after half-time with the score 1–1 the ball broke loose around the centre circle between the City number 4 and the Bury number 5. The odds were in favour of the big strapping Bury defender as he moved in to tackle. The much-lighter City wing-half decided to go for it as well, and due to the fact that he was overstretching, met the ball badly balanced with no weight behind his leg at exactly the same time as his beefy, perfectly balanced opponent. The twangs could be heard streets away. It sounded like a guitar instrumental as every ligament that I knew I possessed snapped, plus a few that I didn't know I had.

I lay there and for a minute I couldn't take it all in. My ankle, my knee—I couldn't decide which was the worst. As I waited for the stretcher I began to get things into perspective among the muddy boots, sky-blue socks, white socks, knobbly knees, cut knees and scarred knees all around me, waiting. This was my worm's eye view as I lay there.

"Is it broken?" one player asked another.

'Oh no,' I thought. I hadn't considered the possibility of the dreaded break, the one injury all players fear most.

"No, it's ligaments, this," said the other.

'Thank God,' I thought, lulled into a false sense of security for a second.

"They are much worse than a break."

'Bloody hell,' I thought.

In the end, somebody had the presence of mind to enquire:

"Where is that damn stretcher? The lad's in agony here."

I heard an old voice shout from the dressing-room door:

"We can't find it."

I thought it was about time I controlled my own destiny. So, hoisting myself up onto my elbow, the pain now almost unbearable, I informed them that the stretcher was outside, propping up the dressing-room wall at the back among the dandelions and overgrown grass where no man had trodden for at least 10 seasons.

Finally it arrived, rusted from the top to bottom due to its exposure to the elements for all those years. Bugs were crawling along the metal frame and as I was lifted onto it my hands sank into two cobwebs as I gripped the sides, ready to be hoisted up and away. There was much grunting and groaning as the old volunteers made their way with me to the sanctuary of the dressing-room. My view of things was as before—a superb view up two pairs of nostrils and the sight of their faces going redder and redder. The only thought in my mind was, 'I hope they don't drop me.'

Polite applause reached my ears as we neared the touch-line. One die-hard squeezed my arm and told me not to worry. Soon I was enveloped in the confines of our dressing-room, the smell of liniment in the air as I lay there, contemplating both my future and how I was going to get dressed. Little did I know that this unglamorous and undignified exit was to be the end of me at Manchester City, my last appearance in my beloved sky-blue shirt. All my dreams, my one single-minded aim in life, was over.

A few weeks later an official-looking envelope dropped through the letterbox of 30 Clough Top Road informing me that I had been given a free transfer. My career at City had ended at exactly the same place it had started: Chassen Road, Urmston.

The Bury number 5, Spike Rawlinson, went on later in life to become a professional comedian and great friend of mine, starring in the night-clubs of his native North-east. He didn't make me laugh that day.

TWO

On the Scrapheap

I WAS NOW IN A PREDICAMENT THAT I HAD NOT envisaged. This situation was definitely not included in my plans—discarded at 19 and struggling to even walk, let alone impress another club enough for them to consider offering me a contract.

At the time, I thought the injury had influenced the club's decision. I now realise that this wasn't so. It had been coming for months previously, only I had been too blind to see it.

One seldom lingers long enough to read one's own graffiti and this had been the case with me. I had missed the tell-tale little signs, like the boss telling me we were playing Newcastle away when really it was Stoke at home. When they started wrapping my boots in a road map I really should have cottoned on, but no, City was my team and although the last few months had been heartbreaking at times, I still had the single-minded thought that I would come through.

There were times when trainer Jim Meadows would organise a practice game and gather the whole playing staff together on the pitch. He'd announce the two teams, handing out shirts to the first team and then announcing the reserve team, who would be providing the opposition. As each name was called, the player would grab a shirt and trot off ready for the game. When this was completed I was the only person left standing there, not knowing what to do because not a word was said to me; if I stayed where I was the game would have to be played around me. I thought this was a particularly harsh way to treat a young player and it happened on a few occasions. Even as I left the scene to knock a ball about in the gym by myself I still couldn't see that, even then, I was on my way out. Oh the folly of youth.

. . .

When, at the tender age of three, I first decided that I would make it my career, I never imagined that such feelings of despair could ever be attached to the game of football. My dad took me along to Maine Road — where else? — to see the legendary Frank Swift, at that time the world's best goalkeeper. 'Big Swifty', always the entertainer, always playing to the crowd but always a great keeper. He was later tragically killed in the Munich air crash of 1958 when the fabulous Manchester United 'Busby Babes' team was decimated.

This day, my first ever game, he was facing the mighty Arsenal. The red shirts with white sleeves were swarming all over City and Swifty was a busy man keeping them at bay. Bert Sproston was playing at full-back with a knee bandage on to support a 'dicky' knee and these were the two players who held my attention as the Gunners beat City three-nil. I decided there and then that this was the life for me and I must one day wear that sky-blue shirt.

With this thought always on my mind to spur me on, I set about kicking my ball in our back garden with much more gusto. Already I had an aim in life. Soon my birthday arrived and my joy knew no bounds when, as I hurriedly ripped open my present, I discovered a green goalkeeper's jersey just like Swifty's. They didn't have sophisticated sports shops in those days and my mother had worked a miracle in converting an old boy scout's jersey into a goalkeeper's ensemble. This didn't matter to me; I never had it off my back.

I was about to start school. My parents encouraged me to go because they said there would be class football matches. At first I went to the very tiny St Mary's in Moston, also in north Manchester. This was the only school that could take me, but from the start my parents tried to get me into a bigger one. There weren't even enough boys to form a football team, so obviously it wouldn't do. My mother and I were also walking about four miles a day to get there and back.

I was quickly moved — my first free transfer — to Crosslee Primary School, nestling behind Blackley's most famous pub, the Clough Hotel. Crosslee was run by an eccentric head-mistress, Miss Helen Stone, who was really a couple of generations ahead of her time. She cycled to school each morning, waving to everyone in sight, left and right, like the Queen. She wore weird clothes, always topped off with a purple beret and matching lipstick. A purple circle the size of a half-crown on each cheek completed the vision — teaching's answer to Margaret Rutherford, and she was loved and respected by everyone.

Teachers were not allowed to smack the pupils at Crosslee but despite being the only school that I was aware of with this policy, the disciplinary record was almost exemplary. None of us ever wanted to let Miss Stone down or be summoned to her office for 'a little chat'.

On my first day there was a class football match in the afternoon. I could hardly wait because I knew I was good at football and even though I didn't know anyone's name I was confident that when I had knocked in a few goals I would soon be popular with the other lads. Come the great event and I never got one single kick of the ball. It was whizzed about at great speed by kids who knew each other, had grown up together, and the whole thing just passed me by. A lad called Victor Boff dominated the whole game, scored goals at will, and at the end of the day it was a shell-shocked little seven-year-old who was met by his mother at home-time.

I had to wait until the same time the following week for my next game. I planned to do considerably better this time round. It was, after all, only a class game but, for me, a Wembley Cup final couldn't have been more important as I mentally prepared myself for the encounter. Thankfully, things went much better as I got into the game from the kick-off and literally dribbled myself stupid as I took on opponent after opponent to rattle in a few goals. The match was watched by Mr Ellison, who, unknown to me, also picked the school team. He was always in the company of the giants of the fourth year so he meant little to me at the time.

Friday at 3pm was always a big day at Crosslee. The whole school would gather in the hall and Miss Stone would take the stage and make all the announcements. This was followed by a deathly hush as she revealed the names of the children who had received an 'order mark'. This was the ultimate in dis-grace at Crosslee and anyone who received one would be avoided and pointed at for weeks as though they were a leper.

After this she turned to the weekend's football fixture. She announced that they would be playing at home against Christ the King School. As each boy's name was called out he had to go to the stage and receive his shirt. The green shirt of Crosslee was a prize I longed for but it was a long way away yet because the team was made up of eleven-year-olds and with me barely seven, four years seemed a long time to wait. She went through the entire team and then said:

"The reserve for tomorrow's game is Fred Eyre."

I couldn't believe it as I got to my feet and made my way shakily up onto the stage to receive my shirt. It felt like gold to me, though actually it was a red one. For some reason the reserve got a red one; maybe it made you appreciate it more when you progressed to the actual team and received a green one.

The applause was still ringing in my ears as I flew out of the school gate and ran all the way home. As kids straggled home I could hear them say, 'That's the kid who is reserve for the school team tomorrow and he's only a first year.' My feet barely touched the ground as I pelted my way home through the prefabs of Colmore Drive. When I got home I insisted that I put the shirt on, 'just to get the feel of it', and run across Blackley to my grandma's house in Belthorne Avenue to show her. It seemed a little big but when I tied up the neck, where there were holes with string through, it didn't flap around too much. Anyway I didn't care what it looked like. As I went to bed that night I was hoping that at least one of the players wouldn't turn up the next day. Manchester City, I'm on my way.

So the great day dawned and my dream came true. The centre-half didn't turn up. After a brief consultation with skipper Barry Skinner, secretly my latest hero (if only I could be as good as him when I got older), it was decided to slot me straight in at centre-half. Even to my young ears I thought this a rather strange decision. Centre-halves were usually the biggest lads who could kick the ball further than anybody else — not little ball players four years younger than everyone else, two feet smaller and two stone lighter. Still, I didn't care. I was going to play, this was the main thing, and I had my number-one fan, my mother, standing shivering on the touch-line to give me confidence.

I must have looked a little out of place as we lined up for the kick-off. I was in my red shirt while the rest of my team-mates wore green. My tensions were not eased when, while waiting for the referee to start the game, someone from the other team spotted me and shouted to his centre-forward, my immediate opponent:

"Hey, have you seen the size of that young kid? When you get near him cart him."

I didn't exactly know what the phrase 'cart him' meant but realised instinctively that it was something unpleasant. 'Get stuck in and hope for the best,' was my thought for the day as we roared to a memorable 4–0 victory. I was overjoyed and went on to play for a record four years, never being left out of the team. Nothing can stop me now.

THREE

On my 'Sweeney' Todd
at Ducie

MY YEARS AT CROSSLEE PASSED QUICKLY. I'D BEEN very happy there but now it was time for the 11-plus examination that would determine where I would spend the next five years of my life. I was one of those borderline cases and had to take the exam again before finally passing.

I had the choice between Ardwick Tech and Ducie Avenue. Both were a long way from my home, so I made a few discreet enquiries among my friends to discover which school had the better football team. This was how I ended up at Ducie.

It was a decision I have never regretted even though the school is set in the heart of Moss Side, one of the less salubrious areas of Manchester where even the alsatians roam about in pairs. It was a big school with a good reputation. Lord Robens, the ex-chairman of the National Coal Board, was a former pupil and my parents were pleased that I was going there, if a little apprehensive of the long journey each morning and night. My dad took the morning off that first day, which proves it was a day of great importance in the Eyre household. I'd not known him take any time off work before. He worked as a butcher for Mr Smalley, who had a shop on

Rochdale Road, Collyhurst, and another which dad ran single-handedly, just off Bradford Road in Ancoats.

We were not a rich family by any means but dad worked hard to make sure we were never short of anything, least of all football boots for me.

My mother took me to the shop every Saturday, a journey requiring three buses, from when I was three years old, so that dad could take me for my weekly dose of football. City one week, United the next—we never missed a match. We would stand in the same spot among the same group of people and I would be passed down to the front over everyone to lean on the wall, perched on a specially made box so I could see over, protected by these massive adults, cheering on my favourites.

How times have changed. It was a wonderful experience to be among the crowd, with none of the obscene chants that you hear today and no hint of violence. Only once in all my years standing behind those goals at the scoreboard end (actually just to the right of the goals because I was tipped off by a stalwart supporter: "Don't stand right behind the goals, son, the players look like chips in a chip pan") did I see any violence. It was on a day when City's Dave Ewing and Everton's Dave Hickson were having a rare old battle and an Everton fan got over-excited and hit someone with his rattle. He was quickly ejected from the ground but such was the rarity of the misdemeanour that it was talked about for seasons to come.

Even at this tender age, I'd seen most of the great players and collected their autographs; I simply lived for weekends. Each Saturday, a big match, while on Sunday I'd board the coach to watch my local team, White Moss Villa, play in the pub league all over Manchester. Maybe if it wasn't City then it could be White Moss Villa when I grew up. Unthinkable— it had to be City.

. . .

Our green Austin 7 drew up outside the large iron gates of Ducie Avenue School. I put my new leather school bag over my shoulders—it was my prize for passing the exam—and prepared to venture into the unknown. I smoothed down my brand-new blazer, looked proudly at my new badge (a giant bee), straightened my school cap and set forth. A very tiny boy, Jon King, was just walking in at the same time and his small stature made me feel a little bolder. We both took deep breaths and marched in together. I had hoped to see him at dinnertime, an ally to spend the hour with, but I couldn't see him anywhere. I was amusing myself by dribbling a stone about on a quiet stretch of playground. I was nicely balanced, head bowed over the ball just like Roy Clarke dashing down the left wing at Maine Road, when all of a sudden a great shadow was cast over me. I thought it was night-time already: I glanced up, thinking, 'I'll stick it through his legs before scoring.' Sixty thousand people were just waiting for me to tap the stone into an empty net after a dribble that had taken me past fourteen defenders—the first four I'd beaten had recovered and come back for a second beating—to score City's winning goal in the last minute. And now my way to goal had been blocked.

I found myself staring into the stomach of a giant sixth-former. A glance to the right and I saw another. A swift look to the left and there was another. I didn't need to look behind to know there were another two behind me.

I raised my sights a little higher to find myself looking into the far-from-pretty face of John Thaw. Perhaps he was already rehearsing for some of the tough-guy roles he would portray in films and on television programmes like *The Sweeney*. His face was grim, with a huge mole over one eye (camouflaged by many a clever make-up artist during his career) which made him look even more fierce.

"Hey, fag."

He spat out the words through tight lips. All first-years were called 'fag' so I didn't mind. Not that I had much choice in the matter.

"Go to the tuck shop and get me a packet of Durex."

I looked in the direction of the tuck shop and saw a quaint, matronly lady selling Arrow bars, Trebor chews, Milky Lunches—but nothing marked 'Durex'. I hesitated a second, then: wham, a dozen pennies wrapped in a handkerchief can be a formidable weapon when crashed down onto the back of your head. It also served as a sharp reminder not to hesitate when Mr Thaw wanted something doing.

I hadn't a clue what a packet of Durex was but knew that you didn't chew them. I was pretty sure you didn't smoke them either. I had no choice but to go and ask for them, so I slowly held out my hand for the money, my brain working overtime because I knew I was in a tricky situation. Fingering the bump that was slowly coming up on the back of my head, I made my way to the tuck shop. I could see Wagon Wheels galore, Mars bars, everything but these damned things.

I decided to hang about inside the shop for a short while before dejectedly coming out shaking my head. The least I'll get, I thought, is another couple of whacks with the pennies.

"She says she's sold out," I announced, inwardly grimacing at the thought of what was to come.

I was in for a pleasant surprise as the five of them turned on their heels roaring with laughter in search of another victim. I was grateful for my narrow escape but my head was thumping after being hit by the pennies. The 'change' didn't do me any good that day, but the experience certainly did.

FOUR

Ducie Bits

DUCIE AVENUE WAS IN MY OPINION A FINE SCHOOL.
The headmaster, Mr Hughes, known affectionately to everyone as 'Sam', was first class, dignified but caring. Most of the
teachers were the same.

The main feature as far as I was concerned was that it
didn't have just one school football team, but three — the
under-12s for the boys in the first and second year, the under-
14s for those in the third and fourth year and the under-16s
for the big lads.

On the first football day, the teacher gathered us all together
and said:

"It's not often anyone gets in the school team in the first
year but those who fancy their chances can stay for trials."

I was there like a shot and we were all sorted out into
positions. Unknown to us, the school team had already
virtually been picked from last year's boys but anyone who
impressed might just sneak in. There were two of us for the
centre-forward spot and, as I might have guessed, the teacher
told the other lad to play there. I made a dive for the right-
wing as my second choice. As the whistle blew, the aspiring
centre-forward set off directly down the centre of the field
punting the ball in front of him while everyone stood and
watched him in amazement. The teacher blew the whistle
and shouted to him:

"You have to pass the ball to somebody else from a kick-off, son."

I stared in disbelief. Here was I, the future captain of England, stuck out on the right wing while the donkey that had taken my place didn't even know the rules of the game.

"Sorry, Sir," he replied as we lined up again.

This time he promptly turned round and booted the ball back to our own startled goalkeeper.

"What have I let myself in for here?"

The ball was brought back and I volunteered to exchange places with him in order to actually set the game in progress. We finally got started. The game had been going precisely two minutes when I picked up a pass just inside my own half, beat two or three players, and shot just wide of the post.

"Oh, shit!" I muttered under my breath, really disappointed at my effort.

"Stop the game. Come here, Eyre."

The teacher beckoned me over. His hearing must be good, I thought. He was at least 50 yards away and I barely uttered the offending words. He's going to send me off, expel me from the school. The colour drained from my face. What will my dad say? I trudged across slowly.

"That's enough for you. Go and join in the other game and have a trial for the under-14s."

My face changed back to its normal colour and I trotted over to the other game. This teacher looked at me, obviously thinking this little 11-year-old had been sent across with some message or other.

"Mr Mitchell says I've to join in this trial, Sir," I announced proudly.

"Oh really, he thinks you're up to it, does he?" he said rather patronisingly.

I didn't really need an extra spur but I remember thinking, 'Just let me get on and I'll wipe that smirk off your face.'

"Where do you want to play?" he asked.

I'd been studying things while I'd been waiting on the touch-line. These were really big lads compared to me, so while I really fancied my usual centre-forward job I thought I'd be safer out of the way.

"Outside-right, please, Sir."

And then I was on.

It was a great feeling being on the same pitch as lads who could really play. When they hit a ball it usually went where they intended it to go. I was on their wavelength and I liked it. It took me a minute or two to realise the difference. The left-winger ran down the line and hammered over a cross to where really I should have been, but I was so used to wingers' crosses not reaching the far post that I never bothered taking up the correct position. I vowed that the next time the winger got clear and put a cross in I would be on the end of it. Shortly after this he broke free again and I galloped in as fast as my little legs could carry me. Over came the cross, over and over it soared, clearing everyone's head as I tried to go even faster to get there and meet it. My head connected just right as I flew horizontally through the air. The ball sailed past the keeper's outstretched hands into the goal. As I was helped to my feet by my new team-mates, I was euphoric.

After the trial, I was in this team as well. A month later, the big lads began their fixtures and I got a game in that team as well. I was going to be a busy boy. It was a good job each team didn't play on the same Saturday or I could have been in trouble. If I kept my place in every team I would be able to represent the school non-stop for the next five years. What a good school this is. It's only the maths, geography etc. that spoils it.

I did in fact play for the next five years and never lost a single match. We had a fantastic team, totally unbeatable, although we did once get one scare when Heald Place held us to a 2–2 draw. A lad called Neil Young caused us a few problems. This was the first time I'd come across Neil but in later years he became a close friend and colleague at City.

Three of us gained Manchester area honours and later Bobby Smith and Dave Latham joined us in trials for the full Manchester Boys team. Five boys from one school — it took some beating.

FIVE

The King of
Boggart Hole Clough

EVERY SPARE MINUTE AT HOME WAS SPENT PLAYING IN
Boggart Hole Clough.

Boggart Hole Clough: I love the very sound of the name.
Until many years later, when I went to Disneyland in the
United States, for me it was the number-one spot in the
world. When you've only been as far as Blackpool you are easily pleased.

I knew every blade of grass and as soon as I was home from
school, and all day Sunday, it was down to the clough. All the
school holidays (it never seemed to rain in those days, of
course) were spent in this vast woodland. People always knew
where to find me. Apart from the pitches there was a lake, a
proper running track — quite a thing in those days — hills to
climb and 'The Hollows' — big crevices with trees of all
shapes and sizes to climb. And, at the bottom, a fairly deep,
muddy, stagnant stream, full of rubbish, old tyres, prams with
wheels missing, the lot. This was our favourite area when we
had a break from the football.

Such affection did this clump of trees hold for us that years
later one of my best schoolboy pals from our Crosslee days
together, Malcolm Roberts — at that time one of Britain's top

singing stars with a record, 'Love Is All', riding high in the charts—came round to see me one afternoon at 30 Clough Top. During our chat he said:

"Do you fancy climbing the Big Oak?"

Two minutes later, a famous singer and a fully grown professional footballer were perched at the top of the Big Oak in the middle of the afternoon, surveying their former kingdom, much to the amazement of the park-keeper who was begging us to come down and 'not be silly'.

. . .

Whit Sunday was, to put it mildly, a bit of a drag. It was the one day of the year when you had to wear your new suit. Parents bought their children Whit Sunday clothes and you would then be sent to show them off to your relatives. Off you would squeak to their homes in your new shoes, standing to attention. Grandma would say:

"Oh, you are a smart boy," and slip a half-crown into your top pocket.

It could be a lucrative day, but what a drag.

"No kicking a ball in those new shoes," my mother would warn me as I left the house to go on my rounds.

I met up with Malc Roberts this particular Whit Sunday. I'd never seen him looking so smart. He was resplendent in new suit, new shirt, tie, everything. His mam had really done him proud. There was nothing to do in Blackley on Whit Sunday, so we decided to hop on the bus to town. We quickly realised that there was nothing to do anywhere on Whit Sunday as we wandered around Manchester. It was like walking through a ghost town. Then it started to rain. We didn't want to get our new clothes wet so we dived into the only place that was open, Manchester Art Gallery. The only thing I knew about painting was when I'd helped my dad paint the kitchen wall. At least we kept our new clothes dry, and that was the main thing.

"What a nice thing to see young people taking an interest in art," a sophisticated voice whispered in our ears.

We both looked round to see a very nice lady obviously so sincere in her comments that we didn't have the heart to disappoint her.

"Yes, we pop down whenever we can between studies," I replied in my poshest accent, thinking this would satisfy her. But her comments became more profound.

"This is a Constable collection, as you probably know," she went on.

"Yes, I love his work," I said knowingly. "I think he should pack the police force in and paint full time, don't you, Malcolm?"

He nodded his head approvingly.

We stopped the joking and were obviously saying the correct things because shortly afterwards she wrote to both our headmasters saying that we were a credit to our schools. It turned out that she was the headmistress at Lily Lane School in Moston and was a close friend of our headmaster, Mr Hughes. She sent us miniature 'Constable' postcards until the day she died. We never had the heart to tell her the truth.

It had brightened up a bit by now so we were off home. As we were walking for our bus we saw, at last, another human being, although to us Mancunians at the time he was regarded as superhuman. It was Brian Statham, the famous Lancashire and England fast bowler, the terror of Australian batsmen. He was walking towards us on Mosley Street. It was too good a chance to miss and we literally bowled him over in our rush to obtain his autograph. We then sat excitedly on the back seat of the 112 bus to the Ben Brierley pub discussing the day and the excitement of getting Brian's signature. The Ben Brierley is a well-known Moston pub which doubled as a bus terminus on the opposite side of Boggart Hole Clough to where we both lived, so we had to walk through the park to get home because the buses were not running any further that day. This was to prove fatal because it meant we had to pass by our favourite haunt, The Hollows.

It was just how we had left it the previous day. Our favourite trees were there of course, looking very inviting, but we managed to resist the urge to climb them. Our thick Tarzan rope was hanging from our tree. When it was pulled up to the top of The Hollows we could swing across the abyss and back again. High above the muddy, rust-filled, stinking, slimy stream we would soar just like Johnny Weismuller. But no, not today, not in our best Whit Sunday clothes.

The rope swung to and fro tantalisingly in the breeze.

"I'll just have one go," I said, and grabbed the rope, running it back up the hill until it was taut.

"Aaaahh," I shouted as I flew through the air and back, to land nimbly on my feet, back where I'd started from.

Malc couldn't resist it either, and with great care he put his piece of paper, with the Brian Statham autograph on it, gently between his teeth — not his lips because he didn't want the paper to get wet or the ink would run. Then he was ready and he set off. High in the air he flew. He was at the peak of his flight when the unbelievable happened—the branch snapped and from about 20 feet in the air Malcolm splashed down into the stagnant morass below him. He plunged like a bird with its wings clipped. He didn't make a splash, more of a splodge, as he almost sank from sight, just his head visible.

An Olympic judge would probably have awarded about 7.8 for technical merit. I awarded it 10 out of 10 as my knees buckled with uncontrollable laughter.

Malc lay flat on his back, all his best Whit-week clothes ruined, with only his head just above the surface. While I tried to regain my composure on top of the hill he shouted to me through clenched teeth that still gripped the precious piece of paper:

"It's all right, don't worry. I managed to keep the autograph dry."

I'm sure Mrs Roberts was pleased to hear that.

SIX

The Dean and I

I WAS NOW BEGINNING TO RELISH THE COMPETITIVE side of football. It was much better than simply training or practising on my own. Saturday was nicely taken care of—school game in the morning, City or United in the afternoon.

On Sunday mornings I went down into the clough to test my shooting ability against Joe Dean. Joe was the current local hero. The Manchester Boys and England Schoolboys goalkeeper had taken over the title of Blackley Boy Makes Good from Wilf McGuinness who had gone through the stages of schoolboy football to captain England Boys and eventually play for Manchester United.

I saw Wilf play most of his games for Manchester Boys. My next-door neighbours, Auntie Alice and Uncle Ernie, took me to the big schoolboy games at Maine Road to cheer him on and he really was an outstanding player. Watching Manchester Schoolboys play at Maine Road had become an annual ritual for us. I remember seeing Dennis Viollet and being almost awe-struck at his ability, thinking, 'God, is this how good you've got to be?' He was an incredible player. So too was Albert Scanlon on the left wing, two years later. Both went on to become famous players for Manchester United. They were two of the Busby Babes who survived the Munich air crash.

Now Joe Dean seemed likely to be the next one to sign for a big club and every Sunday morning he would be like an old-time prize-fighter taking on all-comers, inviting them to try their luck in scoring past him. He was like a colossus, superbly fit — a giant of a youth with huge, safe hands. I used to give my shots everything I had, really concentrating and connecting with some beauties, but just when I thought I'd beaten him an enormous hand would reach out and scoop the ball up with consummate ease. If he was in a little difficulty, four fingers like a plate of sausages would tip my effort around the post.

As the weeks went by my frustrations grew more and more in my attempts to beat him. I would be up early on Sundays with my boots on waiting for him to arrive at about nine-thirty. By twelve-thirty I was on my way back home, dejectedly trudging back for my dinner having failed again. After three hours of non-stop shooting, my legs felt as though I was wearing concrete boots. And I still hadn't managed to put one past him.

This went on for a year until he signed for Bolton Wanderers and not once did I manage to score against him.

In later years I played against him when he kept goal for Bolton Wanderers and never scored, and also when he played for Carlisle United and also never scored. Since we have both retired I have played against him in charity matches many times and still haven't scored. I must beat him at least once before we go to the great Wembley in the sky.

There was, however, a void on Sunday afternoons because there were no games. I could always just go down to the clough to train but really I wanted competitive action.

One particular Sunday we reached an all-time low. I was with my bosom pal Mike Roddy patrolling the streets looking for a game. We were really struggling because disaster had struck; somebody had pinched our ball. Imagine, Sunday afternoon and no ball. We were like a couple of stray tomcats in search of scraps as we covered Blackley in need of a game. Eventually we saw a particularly obnoxious kid sat in his bedroom window. This lad was not one of our gang. We disliked him intensely, but one thing in his favour was that he always had all the gear. In the summer he would not only have wickets but bails as well, a corky with a seam, proper wicket-keeping gloves and his bat was a 'three-springer'. We thought his dad must be a bank robber. We had a piece of wood and a tenniser (tennis ball) with a lamp-post for wickets and the first crack in the pavement was the crease. When we went to the baths we didn't have trunks. Unlikely as it may sound now, we had a 'V' neck Fair Isle pullover instead. We'd slip our legs through the arm-holes, hold it up with a snake belt, and dive in. When we hit the water it would hold in the wool, weigh us down, and finish round our ankles, exposing ourselves to the world. This kid, Dennis, had flippers, snorkel and goggles.

Our hopes for a game rose when we spied him this day. It was a bit of a sacrifice to allow him to play with us, but we quickly weighed things up and felt it was worth putting up with him. It was the least we could do.

"Dennis," I shouted up to him, feeling like the lead actor in the balcony scene from *Romeo and Juliet*.

"Are you coming out to play? And bringing your ball?"

Dennis, amazed by his sudden rise in the popularity stakes, shouted down enthusiastically:

"Yes, I'm coming out. But my ball's burst."

"See you, Dennis," came the reply as Mike and I wended our weary way.

Then, with a flash of genius I came up with the answer to fill our Sunday afternoons. We will form a team of our own. If we have our own team we will never be short of a game, I reasoned. It was the ideal solution and I, of course, would assume the role of player-manager, penalty taker, corner-kick taker, taker of the throw-ins, free kicks, and anything else that was going. How could we go wrong? So I became a manager for the first time at the age of 12.

I soon recruited the best players in Blackley and challenged anybody foolish enough to pass through the district. We had a good team, with relatively few selection problems. It was simple: my best mates played in whichever of the other 10 positions they fancied (the number 9 shirt was reserved exclusively for me) and those further down my social roster had what was left. I don't know why the professional managers make such a big fuss about the job.

At times disciplinary action had to be taken. On one occasion a team-mate said he would get me a Blackpool programme because he was going to stay at his Grandma's who lived at the seaside. He forgot, so was promptly axed from the team for the next match. You've got to be firm with these players. Especially after a serious indiscretion such as this.

SEVEN

White Hart-break Lane

AS A RESULT OF ALL MY OUT-OF-SCHOOL ACTIVITY, MY football was improving enormously. Unfortunately the same could not be said about my school-work. When the time came to streamline my subjects it was a difficult decision because I was poor at them all.

I decided to take commerce, my reasoning being that when I had completed my career as a star footballer, a knowledge of commerce, however scant, would stand me in good stead for the day I took the customary newsagent's shop. It was all figured out, but Mr Castley, our commerce teacher, was not so confident. During our lessons my mind would wander to the next game and try as I might, I could not concentrate on my school-work.

I found it particularly hard this Wednesday afternoon in 1957 when City had a vital FA Cup replay and were kicking off at 2.15pm. They had drawn at Newcastle on the Saturday and today was replay day. What I would have given to have been there. I toyed with the idea of 'becoming ill' on the big day but this idea was quickly removed from my mind when the teacher said to me the day before:

"Even if you are feeling half dead, I advise you to come in tomorrow because yours is the first face I shall be looking for."

Ah, the price of fame.

I had to content myself with a place at my desk, calculating the score by the loudness of the roars. My ears were like decibel meters as I followed the game kick by kick. A few near misses, one or two 'Ooo's and an odd 'Aah'. Then four o'clock came — home time. The game had been over five minutes and as I came out of school I caught the first of the supporters on their way home. They, I was sure, would disprove my calculations that City had lost 5–4. What a ridiculous score. Who could beat City 5–4 at home, in the Cup as well? Out of the question. I had obviously read the roars wrongly.

I raced down Denmark Road and shouted to the first man I saw decked out in sky blue and white:

"What was the score, Mister?"

"We lost 5–4," came the reply.

My calculations were correct; if only I was as good in the maths lessons.

"Newcastle brought in a lad at centre-forward called Alex Tait. Never heard of him before. Red hair just like you, and he scored a hat-trick."

No Wembley for me this year, then. It was the one time in my life that I'd wanted to be proved wrong.

· · ·

The trials for Manchester Boys came round and the school sent five of us. It was a tremendous honour to play for Manchester Boys. If you made the team you were under constant scrutiny by the top clubs and indeed a host of famous players had reached the top after playing for them. Finally, from the thousands of boys, a squad of eighteen was announced including two from our school, my mate Bob Smith and myself.

Football had brought Bob and I together. He had missed the whole of the first year's schooling and also the all-important trials for the school team, so he had been a late starter. If it hadn't been for me he may have been a non-starter. Because of all the time he had off school with illness the teachers didn't know if he was any good or not. Being a fellow North Manchester lad, I had seen him perform in the clough and was able to put in a good word with the teacher. Now he was making up for lost time.

We were both selected for the opening fixtures, him at right-back and me in front of him at right-half. We were two ginger nuts together although he insists to this day that his is auburn. Both strands.

The team remained unchanged as we won all our games. My eyes were set firmly on 'The Big One' in a week's time, away to London Boys, when I would achieve another of my ambitions and play on a Football League ground for the first time.

The game was to be played at White Hart Lane, the home of Tottenham Hotspur. Under floodlights as well: a wonderful experience. First, we had to dispose of St Helens Boys on Saturday, before leaving for London on Tuesday to stay overnight in London, play the game at night and return home the next day. Just like a proper footballer. I'd better get used to this if it was going to be my life for the next 15 years.

Secretly I had not been happy with my form. The selectors seemed pleased enough, though. I was picked for all the games and we had won them handsomely with me in the side. This reassured me and I kept pushing my fears to the back of my mind.

The problem was that something I had wanted badly all my life was now within my grasp. A final push and I would be there—offered a job on the ground staff of some club, hopefully City. All I had to do was play well. I was a good player, I knew that. I was as good, if not better, than most of the other players in the team, with an excellent, almost unparalleled playing record behind me. But I was becoming too anxious. I couldn't relax when the day of the game came round. My old carefree, confident style wasn't really there. I was trying too hard to impress the all-seeing eyes of the 'scouts' who were watching. I was my own most difficult opponent. While I played tensely, others with less skill were performing with carefree abandon and playing well. The main thing was that we were winning, so I believed a couple more games would allow me to relax and enjoy myself. Roll on White Hart Lane.

Before boarding the coach for the trip to St Helens I had gone to Littlewoods with my mother to choose my first holdall.

"You'll have to have one for all those overnight stays you'll be having from now on," she said.

I chose a smashing blue one—no other colour would do. She took it home to pack my gear for London while I went to fight the foe at St Helens.

The coach arrived at the school in St Helens, ironically in a street called Frederick Street, and I tried to convince myself that this was a good omen as I did battle with my nerves again. I thought I was succeeding and appeared outwardly calm, laughing and singing all the Everley Brothers hits with the boys when, 'Whoosh'. I thought somebody had tipped a bowl of tomato soup over me as my lap filled up with blood. It cascaded from my nose like Niagara Falls, completely ruining my clothes.

"Don't tell Whetton," I whispered to Bob, who had by this time dived out from the seat next to me to avoid any splashes ruining his brand-new suit, a delicate little number from 'Damien's, Tailors of Distinction' on Moston Lane. A few red dots would have completed his ensemble nicely.

Mr Whetton was the team manager and the most miserable man I had ever met until then. Or since then, come to think of it. My lace had come undone during one game and I managed to tie it, just in time to score the winning goal for Manchester Boys. I was met by a volley of abuse from him as I got back to the dressing-room for not being able to tie my boots properly. The goal never got a mention. He was now sitting at the front of the coach with his number two, Cain. What a pair. I was sure if he heard of my predicament I would be out of the team, so I quickly wrapped my gabardine around me to cover up the mess and hurried into the dressing-room. What with my nerves and my nose, I was in a fine mess. Just let me get through the game.

I was fast losing sight of the most important thing — that football is a game to enjoy. Take it seriously by all means, but above all enjoy it.

In future years as I became a coach myself and dealt with hundreds of young kids on trial, I would always try to relax them early on, telling them they were under no pressure.

"Don't try to impress me." I would say. "Just do your best and enjoy yourself."

I certainly wasn't enjoying myself this day. I was just about getting through, a little bit here, a little bit there. Bob behind me was having a storming game, constantly surging forward on overlaps, years before they were even invented. I was doing a useful little job covering the gaps he left. At the final whistle we had won 4–0 and I was pleased that the game was out of the way. I'll make London Boys suffer on Wednesday instead.

We were all in high spirits as the coach chugged its way back to Manchester down the East Lancs Road. For the entire journey Whetton and Cain had been huddled together on the front seat like a couple of secret agents. Finally, he silenced us between choruses of 'Bird-dog' and 'Singing The Blues', as he came down the aisle of the bus with a crumpled scrap of paper in his hand, his drooping moustache twitching.

"This is the team for the game against London."

He began to trot out the familiar names: Brian Greenhalgh in goal, Joe Clayton right-back. I didn't believe it; Bob had been dropped. I thought he'd had a great game. I glanced at him quickly in the seat next to me. He looked grim. Left-back Peter Jackson, right-half Bob Smith — relief on Bob's face. I must be left-half, I thought. I'd played there before. Poor old Mike Rabbitt was going to be out of the side as I was switched to left-half. Rabbitt and Eyre — what a pair of wing-halves we made, a couple of 'Bunnies'. We didn't get measles, we got myxomatosis. Centre-half Alan Atherton, he went on. Left-half Mike Rabbitt. My heart sank to my boots. O-U-T. What a blow. In the next few seconds I managed to pull myself together sufficiently to convince everyone that I had taken it well. I'd never been to London anyway, I consoled myself, so it would be a nice couple of days' holiday. And maybe somebody would fall ill.

"The following players are travelling reserves."

Again my name was missing. I was, for the first time in my life, completely shattered — a feeling I was to get to know many times in the future.

How they could leave me out of the squad when I had played in every minute of every game and take the five reserves, none of whom had even kicked a ball for the team. It was just too much for me to comprehend. I got off the coach in Piccadilly. Not a word had been said to me by Whetton or Cain. I walked down Market Street like a zombie and nipped into the first back alley, Cromford Court, and was physically sick down the nearest grid.

The journey home on the bus seemed to take a lifetime. My dad opened the door of number 30. I brushed aside his usual first question of, "How did you get on?" and collapsed on to the settee and cried for an hour. I was never picked to play for Manchester Boys again.

Being the true sportsman I am, I hoped that they would get hammered 5–0 and that Whetton would be crawling round to our house admitting a severe error of judgement and would I please, please, play for Manchester Boys in all their remaining fixtures.

I was sitting on the stairs the morning after the game, waiting to catch the *Daily Express* before it hit the floor to find out the score. There was a good picture of Ernie Ackerley scoring the fifth in a 'Superb 5–0 win for Manchester Boys'. I was glad for my mates but sad inside. Players throughout the world over will know the mixed emotion. It's only natural, I hope.

Bob, who took my place, went on to play for Lancashire Boys and England Boys, at Wembley, God bless him. I don't know how but he's still my oldest friend to this day. He certainly made up for that lost time. He was kind enough to bring me back the programme, with my name on the team-sheet listed as playing right-half. I still have it to this day. I would have been playing against Martin Peters; what a narrow escape for him. I could have destroyed his confidence and ruined his career. England might not have won the World Cup. Perhaps the nation should be proud of me.

My main problem now was how would I get taken on by a league club when I wasn't being watched playing for Manchester Boys. It was back to the clough for me. Back to the drawing board.

EIGHT

Sent for Trial

BLACKLEY LADS HAVE ALWAYS BEEN BLESSED WITH spirit. Les Dawson, who lived behind the shops near me, struggled for years as a small-time comedian and piano player in working-men's clubs all over the north of England and in dives and places of ill repute in Paris, but his Blackley spirit kept him plugging away until he was finally successful.

The same with Bernard Manning. He knows the meaning of the word graft. He used to sing at night for the big bands and help run the family greengrocery business by day.

My old hero, Wilf McGuinness, after scaling the heights for Manchester United and gaining a full England cap, plunged into the depths with a broken leg of such severity that it finished his career as a player. But only after he'd made super-human efforts to make a comeback. He typified the Blackley spirit.

Now it was my chance to prove that I was up there with the best of them. I'd done it before, even though I knew nothing about it at the time. The doctors thought I was 'a goner' as a baby after I'd contracted double pneumonia and pleurisy. For about three months my cot was left downstairs in the warm where mum slept by my side night after night on the settee. Even then I proved that I was a true Blackley baby, pulling through with much nursing from anxious parents.

I was a big boy now, and after the initial shock had worn off and I started eating again, I threw myself into my training even harder than before. As well as my ball-work in the clough, I devised a set of exercises and a little circuit to do every evening in the kitchen when I got home from school. This entailed press-ups, trunk curls on the kitchen floor and step-ups on the kitchen chair, all performed while my mother was preparing the tea. During this time she also became pretty nifty on her feet, as she learned to avoid my prostrate grunting body with amazing dexterity. At the end of my 15-minutes circuit I would be covered in sweat. I didn't realise this was due to the steam from the pressure cooker until we had a salad for tea one night and I wasn't sweating when I'd finished my circuit.

I kept this routine going all through the season, right through to Cup Final Day. Cup Final Day was, and still is — despite clubs treating it less seriously these days — one of the main events of the 'Fred Eyre Social Calendar'. I love everything about Cup Final Day. The weather is invariably beautiful. The players, no matter how hard a season they have had, always look in peak condition. They have new kit especially for the occasion, fresh and clean. The ground is filled to capacity. The turf is lush and green, the stripes seemingly cut with slide-rule precision And the community singing is fantastic. It typifies the spirit of the game to hear, 10 minutes before the kick-off, both sets of supporters singing 'Abide With Me' in unison — together, then as soon as the whistle blows, cheer your own team on.

Every Cup Final Day, Uncle Gus would come in from next door. For as long as I could remember Uncle Gus had been of bad health. I can't ever remember him working. He was stuck indoors all day wheezing and coughing, and we all knew he'd die shortly. In fact, we feared that he would die this particular night. It was lashing down with rain (it always is during an emergency) when one of his daughters rushed to our house to say if he didn't have a tablet within 30 minutes he would die, and they hadn't any left.

At that time we were the only family in Clough Top Road with a car to make the necessary journey to the all-night Boots in town. Dad grabbed his coat and dashed out in the monsoon to the little car parked at the kerb, trying to put his coat on as he ran. One arm in, a quick swing round the shoulders and clink, the keys flew out of his pocket and slithered along the gutter. Before they even reached the grid I could see from the doorway what was going to happen. We stood transfixed as slither-slither, plop, right down the drain they went.

My poor dad was already blaming himself for Uncle Gus's death. Visions of the funeral flashed before our eyes. Down he went, with his face in the gutter trying to get his hand through the narrow iron slats. No chance. Only I could do it. I got my whole arm in, right up to my shoulder, but as I fingered among the slime, torrential rain beating down on my back, my right ear ploughing a furrow through the mud, I couldn't get the keys. Eventually after much rooting about and scooping, I came up with the treasure and Uncle Gus was granted a few more Cup finals.

He had four daughters who knew nothing about football, so he would come in to watch with us. We would get the shandies ready, a quarter of chocolate caramels, draw the curtains and never move from the TV set until the last player had disappeared down the tunnel after the lap of honour. We must have looked an unlikely duo, but it was something I always remember with great affection.

City had been to Wembley twice, of course, in 1955 and 1956. My dad and me had hardly missed a game since he started taking me to Maine Road at the age of three, but there was absolutely no chance of us getting two tickets for either final. We had bought a little black-and-white TV set with a 12-inch screen in time to watch the first one against Newcastle and it was heartbreaking for me to see them lose after Bobby Johnstone had given us fresh hope with that magnificently headed goal just before half-time. This came after the double setback of conceding a first-minute goal and also the blow of losing Jimmy Meadows with a serious injury to his knee. This gave Newcastle's Bobby Mitchell just the time and space he needed to cause havoc among City's patched-up defence and he quickly seized the opportunity to lay on a goal for little George Hannah and also to notch one up for himself.

In later years, I was to play against both Bobby Johnstone and Bobby Mitchell, and I have to say that I hardly covered myself with glory on either occasion. Mitchell was a mercurial left-winger for Newcastle in the early 1950s when the FA Cup almost became their property and the Geordies seemed to monopolise Wembley Stadium. He was the mainspring behind nearly every Newcastle attack spanning about 10 seasons and his magic invariably ended in goals for Jackie Milburn, George Robledo or Vic Keeble.

I played against him at Redheugh Park instead of St James' Park, and in the North Regional League not the Football League. All the same, the telltale features were still in evidence as I watched the opposition shooting in before the game. The hair was still wavy, although there was not quite as much of it. He was a little heavier around the thighs and girth, but the left foot was as sweet as a nut as he fired shots at his goalkeeper, who looked young enough to be his son. Yes, it was him alright. I could only see him from the back, still wearing the familiar number 11. It was now the white shirt of Gateshead and not the famous black-and-white stripes of Newcastle United. The style and grace were unmistakable. I could not imagine how old he was, but it was definitely Bobby Mitchell. I was mesmerised. I was back at Wembley. There he was, dancing and prancing his way along the touch-line, crossing endless balls into City's over-worked penalty area.

The sound of the referee's whistle brought me back to earth, back to Gateshead Football Club. Centre-forward Frank McKenna rolled the ball the customary couple of yards to his inside-left, Steele, who, in one movement, swept the ball out to Mitchell wide on the left touch-line. I had lined up about 50 yards away in the left-half position, but startled everybody by sprinting across the entire width of the pitch. Before Bobby Mitchell could get into his shuffling stride, I hit him with the most horrendous tackle that it has ever been my misfortune to perpetrate. I can remember the mixture of old age, horror, shock and downright disbelief on his face as I clattered into him and left him in a tangled heap on the floor. His pension book flew out of his back pocket. Outraged officials leapt from the bench. My own manager buried his head in his hands. And, as I stood over him, the red mist began to clear from my eyes.

It has to be said that Bobby Mitchell, lying in a crumpled heap at my feet, was, as well as being a truly great player, also a gentleman footballer who, in a matter of seconds, had managed to regain both his composure and his dignity. Instead of reacting equally violently, as he was fully entitled to do, he looked up at me like a homeless bloodhound, blinked his doleful eyes with bags under them as big as John Wayne's saddle-bags, and, with a light Scottish lilt in his voice, asked gently:

"What was that for?"

By now my head had cleared completely. I was that nice lad with good manners from Crosslee School once more. As I surveyed the wreckage, I felt a mixture of stupidity and inadequacy as I mumbled:

"Dunno. For 1955, I suppose."

He looked at me as if I was the village idiot, someone to be pitied. He sighed a little and held out his hand for me to help him shakily to his feet. His action probably saved me from the ignominy of the quickest sending-off on record. We then tried to get on with the game.

This sort of thing happened to me only once before, when I found myself playing against Bobby Johnstone at Oldham Athletic. Bobby was a fantastic footballer. He was bought by City from Hibernian, supposedly to replace Don Revie, who was having another dispute with the club. I went to see Johnstone's first appearance in a pre-season game at Maine Road: Blues against Maroons (first team against reserves) and I could not believe his skill. In fact, after he had scored past reserve keeper John Savage, the big man turned to us all standing behind the goals and said it was best goal he had ever seen, let alone had scored against him.

I was still only 10 years old, but I could tell that Johnstone was something special. He was a Scottish international, born in Selkirk and had been one of the Hib's Famous Five — Gordon Smith, Bobby Johnstone, Lawrie Reilly, Eddie Turnbull and Willie Ormond. He was brilliant during his spell at Maine Road. A little portly and reported to like a drink or three, he nevertheless produced the goods on the field where it matters and scored a goal in each of City's FA Cup final appearances. Eventually he moved along the road to Oldham Athletic where he, more than anyone, helped to revitalise an ailing club and put them on the football map, long before Joe Royle came along.

By the time I came into contact with him, Bobby was playing the game by memory but, unfortunately for me, didn't suffer from amnesia this day at Boundary Park. He proceeded to play round me as if I wasn't there. I had seen him play for so long from the terraces that I was finding it difficult to break the habit and I was now enjoying watching him perform from close quarters. He never broke sweat during the first 45 minutes and, if he did, I wasn't near enough to detect the aroma of Tetley's best bitter. As he ambled about the midfield in his blue-and-white-halved jersey, his passing was like radar (those quaint Oldham shirts of the day were probably the only halves that Bobby Johnstone ever had). It was 3–0 at half-time. Johnstone had scored two and laid on the other one. I trooped into the dressing-room with the rest of the lads for the usual cuppa and a bollocking.

The dressing-room door closed behind the last man in and all was strangely quiet. Everyone seemed to be staring in my direction. It was obvious what they were thinking so, being a bright quick-thinking Blackley lad, I decided that, unlike the previous 45 minutes, attack was definitely the best form of defence.

"Don't all look at me." I protested. "I was nowhere near him when he scored his two goals."

As soon as I had uttered the words, I realised that I hadn't quite got it right.

"Precisely," I was told in no uncertain terms. "Is there any possible chance that you might get somewhere near him during the next 45 minutes?"

Johnstone was a great player to watch, though.

City did get to Wembley again, in 1969, but I had been and gone by then. I was back with my shandy and caramels watching as my pal Neil Young smashed the game's only goal past Peter Shilton to beat Leicester City. If it couldn't be me, then I was glad it was him.

However, this particular Cup Final Day, Nottingham Forest had just beaten Luton Town and the spectacle of the day had made me eager for a game, so I rounded up Mike Roddy and it was down to the clough as usual.

The game was in full flow. I remember I was feeling particularly perky when my dad appeared from the bushes. This was very strange, he never came down to the clough; it must be something very important.

"You had better get back up to the house, there's somebody from City to see you."

The words I had waited 15 years to hear. I grabbed my coat, leaving the lads a goalpost short, and dashed back home.

Enjoying a cup of coffee with my mother was the figure of Harry Godwin in a check overcoat, smart shirt and tie — a fine representative of the club.

Harry was a super person, ideal for the job of scout for a club like City and to make things even better, a Blackley man. He has been responsible for signing most of City's young stars over the years: Peter Barnes, Gary Owen, Mike Doyle, Neil Young, Dave Wagstaffe, Paul Power, Glyn Pardoe, Alan Oakes and a host of others who went on to become top names in the game. Surely with a record like that he can be forgiven for making one mistake, because now he was wanting to sign me—or was he? While I was wondering where my best pen was (I wanted to sign in my best writing) Harry was quietly pouring a little cold water on my enthusiasm. The majority of my former team-mates had by this time been offered ground-staff contracts with the big clubs. Bob Smith, Dave Latham and Ernie Ackerley had signed for United, Ken Fletcher and Neil Young for City and so on.

"But due to the fact that you weren't in the Manchester Boys team for such a long spell," Harry went on, "the best we can offer you is a trial."

'A trial? Bloody hell,' I thought. 'I'm going to have to prove myself all over again.'

And I knew inwardly I was not at my best when I was subjected to that sort of pressure, and was able to perform much better when I was at ease with the world. But I had two choices, 'Take it or leave it.' I took it, shook Harry's hand at the door and watched him walk briskly up Clough Top until his muscular frame disappeared round the corner at the top. As I turned back into the house I was met by huge smiles and grins of well-done by my mam and dad. Only for me to ungratefully return them with a grim, tight-lipped:

"Flippin' trial."

The day of reckoning came when I had to report for my trial at 6pm on August 4th 1959 at Shawe View Field, Chassen Road, Urmston. It was a glorious day, the sun shining incessantly the whole day long. We were in the middle of our summer holidays. Everyone was outdoors breathing in the wonderful fresh air, everyone except me. I stayed in bed the whole day reading and conserving my energy, wrongly reasoning that I would unleash it all on the other unsuspecting trialists that evening.

Chassen Road was two bus rides and a train journey away but I seemed to be there in no time and I walked in with my gear to be met by the first of a breed of men who were to play an important part in my soccer life in the future — the coach. His name was Jimmy Meadows and he was the first in a line of 82 coaches whose job it was at one stage or another to shape my career. Together with my 29 managers it makes a hell of a lot of bosses.

Coaches

EXCLUDING THE MANAGER LES MCDOWELL AND ASSISTANT
manager George Poyser, there were seven coaches at
Manchester City when I arrived. More than Finglands, the
coach firm that took us to away games.

This evening back at Urmston I was to be spoken to by a
coach for the first time in my life and I was already convinced
that I would go home a better player. The coach was Jimmy
Meadows. Jim had come to City as a right-winger from
Southport but was successfully converted to full-back and
gained an England cap. Unfortunately he sustained a serious
knee injury in the 1955 FA Cup final defeat by Newcastle
United which cost City the Cup and his playing career came
to an abrupt end.

Now he was in charge of the young kids and I took an
immediate liking to him, but like most of the other lads I
was a bit frightened of him. He was always very good to me
but I made sure I never stepped out of line. My fears in this
direction were confirmed when, later in the season, Dave
Shawcross, a highly talented wing-half, had the nerve to give
Jim a bit of back-chat. 'Shawcy' was in the bath at the time,
wallowing like a contented hippo, lathering himself with
soap. Jim appeared in the doorway after hearing the remark.
Shawcy took one look at Jim's face, leapt from the bath and

ran through the dressing-room. He hared down the players' tunnel completely naked, soap suds streaming from his body, and then across the pitch with Jim racing in pursuit. Jim's bad leg was temporarily forgotten and he brandished his fist like a side of ham. Shawcy's fitness was the key factor, together with his fear, which gave him extra impetus as he ran the length of the field, past startled ground-staff men who were casually forking the pitch. Over the wall, up the terraces, then he clambered up the rickety steps into the sanctuary of the scoreboard and locked himself in. Jim finally arrived on the scene and positioned himself at the foot of the ladder to wait until the shivering Shawcy decided to give himself up. It was a funny sight to see Dave's head poking through the squares where usually the half-time scores were displayed, trying to figure a way out: Jim 1, Shawcy 0.

(Ironically Shawcy's career went the same way as Jim's—England Under-23 cap, then a serious knee injury that ruined his career after he collided with Wolves keeper Malcolm Finlayson at Molineux.)

In that first-ever session, we sat round Jim cross-legged in a circle on the floor. He looked like an Adonis standing over us in his blue tracksuit and his first words will live with me for ever.

"You can all sit closer to me than this, I've not got shit on my shoes."

Not a bad start. Things could only improve after this. And they did. I settled down well. I always found Jim a hard taskmaster but he was fair with me, which was to be a rarity with coaches and managers, as I was to find out over the years.

There were over 1,000 trialists passing through the

dressing-rooms of Chassen Road in the next six weeks, of which two were signed as amateurs. One of them left two weeks after he signed, so that left just me — one in 1,000. I'll never forget the day when I signed, leaning on the window ledge of Harry Godwin's house on Victoria Avenue — in Blackley, it had to be. Still not a full ground-staff contract but it was a start. Maybe if I impressed in the games I would be offered a contract.

I felt confident of improving under the whip of Jim and the gentle touch of Dick Niellson, but never got the chance. A reshuffle of the ranks at the club found Jim promoted to first-team coach in place of Laurie Barnett, who moved over to be physio. Laurie had been at the club a lifetime. He was a former full-back who was now getting on in years. He was deaf and if he didn't want to be bothered with anything he would simply switch off his hearing aid. He had seen it all and his lack of enthusiasm and dour exterior didn't really endear him to the rest of the players. I received one single piece of advice from Laurie during the entire time I was at the club — which was a few years — and I saw him every morning and almost every afternoon.

"Get to the pitch of the ball."

That was it. I thought he meant the pitch that we were playing on.

Fred Tilson, the reserve-team trainer, was even worse. He sat all day in his little room picking horses and sleeping. I used to go back for extra training in the afternoons and would have a hard job waking Fred at about two o'clock for him to open the gym for me. The rattle of his keys was drowned by his moaning. Fred was a legend at City. He'd scored two goals in the 1934 Cup final and this seemed to ensure him a job for life. I also received just one piece of advice from him in all my time there:

"You should have your bleedin' tonsils out," he informed me in his thick Barnsley accent, after I complained one day of yet another sore throat.

Jim McLelland, an elderly Scottish gentleman, was the 'A'-team coach at the time. He was assisted by a part-timer, Joe Mycock, who used to smoke a pipe like Popeye and tell us jokes in the dressing-room before we took the field. Jim also gave me a pearl of wisdom when he got all of us ground-staff lads together and informed us that football was 'like a wortch', said in a gentle, lilting Scottish accent, 'If one part isn't working it falls out of gear.' We all nodded appreciatively, though none of us could follow the reasoning. The phrase 'like a wortch' became part of our vocabulary to describe absolutely anything.

"How's your ankle?"

"Well, it's like a wortch."

Jim was a kind person, but not really strong enough to cope with the lads.

The two other part-timers, Dick and Walt, I liked very much. They were warm and kind but quite firm without ever dampening your spirit or enthusiasm. The fact that Dick did the job for so long is a testimony to the quality of the man.

Finally there was Johnny, Johnny Hart. I desperately wanted to like Johnny and for him to like me, but he made it terribly difficult for me to warm to him in the early days. Secretly I had always admired him as a player and when he was in a good mood I appreciated his dry sense of humour, but I never knew where I was with him from one day to the next. One day joke after joke tripped off his tongue, the next he would totally ignore me. I simply couldn't read his moods at all.

John hated to lose at anything, not a bad trait to possess. One day Jim Meadows and himself challenged Neil Young and me to a game of doubles at table tennis for sixpence per man. John always won; snooker, billiards, table tennis, head tennis, skittle ball. You name it, John was always the winner. But this day Neil and me were going quite well and the word spread around the club that Jim and John were in danger of losing a tanner each. The mere thought was inconceivable and soon the table-tennis room was filled to capacity as the whole club cheered every point Neil and I won and hissed and booed every time Jim or John scored a lucky point. A huge roar went up as Neil smashed in the winning backhand and everybody waited to witness the momentous occasion when Jim and John would actually hand over the money.

Jim laughed and tossed Neil a tanner. John scowled at me and without a word, bent down and slid the coin firmly along the floor until it came to rest right in the middle of the floor underneath the table-tennis table.

"If you want it you'll have to crawl on your hands and knees to get it," he said over his shoulder as he left the scene. John knew how to make me suffer.

So they were my coaches, together with the manager Les McDowell, who was always conspicuous by his absence. And we didn't see much more of his assistant 'Genial' George Poyser, who smoked his pipe so much it had worn all his teeth away. George, it seemed, used to spend most of his time playing snooker and eating egg butties. Typically, I also received my customary single piece of advice from him while I was recovering from a pulled muscle:

"Play wi' it while you're watching TV at home," he advised.

I presume he meant my leg.

It has to be said that a lot of players made the grade during this period, but I feel they made it in spite of the system, not because of it. There were others who needed a bit of help along the way, a bit of guidance, as we took the wrong track. If we had received it at the correct time, we would have done much better. Maybe we still wouldn't have reached the top but I think that we could have done much better.

. . . .

After my introduction to coaches at City I came across some classic cases during my career. One said to me before a game at Grimsby:

"I want you to do a pacific job for me today."

I don't think I endeared myself to him by replying:

"Well you'll have to give me oceans of room then."

They say things with the best intentions but just can't seem to get it right.

Our coach at Bradford said:

"Fred, I want you to play today like you've never played before — I want you to play well."

I knew what he meant, it just didn't do me much good on the day.

They are usually at their best at half-time when things are

not quite going to plan.

"Too many of our square balls are going through the middle," one screamed at us at Scunthorpe during the break.

In one of my teams we had a player alongside me in the back four who had a bad stammer. I used to make a few bob off him on the coach, playing snap for money! For some inexplicable reason the boss put him in charge of our offside trap. Before he could shout, 'O,o,——uut' we'd be a goal down. In the end he asked the boss to 'relieve him of the re-re-re-responsibility'. I used to take the mickey out of him a bit about his stammer, so much so that one day he turned to me and said:

"I'm s-sorry I ever told you I ha-had a blo-bloody stammer."

I couldn't believe it when in later years he became a manager. If ever there was anyone less suited to be a manager it was him. I believed it even less when he made me his first signing.

"If y-you f-fancy signing g-give m-me a r-ring at home. If nobody answers that w-will be m-me," he said.

I think I signed out of curiosity and he didn't let me down. Before one game he said:

"We're not playing 4–3–3 today. I'm scrapping it and we're playing a new system. We'll have four at the back the same as before, three up front the same as before, but only two in midfield and you, Fred, I want you to play in between the two."

It sounded very much like 4–3–3 to me but, after all, he was the manager.

Another superb example of coaching and attention to

detail was the day we kicked off at 6.15pm during the power shortage in the early 1970s to save the expense of floodlights. At seven o'clock we were all sitting in the dressing-room at half-time, boots caked with mud, mud-stained shirts and shorts, sweat-soaked faces, ball marks in the centre of foreheads where we had occasionally headed one correctly. Steaming cups of tea were held in 10 pairs of grubby, muddy hands (I was the odd one out, I don't drink tea). A player was on the treatment table having his gashed knee cleaned up. We were on the receiving end of a severe bollocking from our coach because we were losing 0–1 at home.

The door opened, stopping our coach in full flight, and the senior coach came in and took over, ending up by wishing us all good luck. We gently pointed out that we didn't usually sweat so much while simply drinking tea and he sheepishly had to admit he'd thought it was a 7pm kick-off.

He went one better later in the season when we played a cup-tie against much stronger opposition away from home. His plan was 'to contain them right from the kick-off'. We would pull every man back, man-for-man mark, play a sweeper behind the sweeper, and employ every defensive tactic in the book to ensure a nil-nil draw and a replay. With these instructions firmly in our heads, we left the dressing-room.

We lost the toss and kicked off. Straight from the kick-off the ball was knocked out to our right-winger, who beat two men on the flank, got to the by-line, put over a picture cross and, much to our delight, it was headed gleefully into the net by our number 10. Amid our jubilation I looked across to the dug-out. He was laughing:

"Can't you do anything I tell you? You've ruined the entire plan. You're on your own now for the next 88 minutes. Don't look to me for any more help."

We eventually lost 1–2. He said at the end:

"What do you expect if you don't follow my instructions?"

But all that was in the future.

TEN

A Mars a Day Helps You Work, Rest and Play

I FELT MY GAME IMPROVING PLAYING AGAINST quality opposition every week. I had appeared in every game and was now quite used to the surroundings at 'Hatters Park', the little ground behind a pub in Denton where we played. Still, there was no mention of a proper contract. This was particularly frustrating because, by now, school-work was really beginning to get me down.

I had just finished a feast of a tea this horrible wet evening in mid-October and was slumped in a chair watching Eamon Andrews make a fool of himself in *Crackerjack* when I glanced at the evening paper. In very minute type at the foot of the sports page it read: 'Tonight's Fixture at Maine Road, Representative Match, Manchester *v* Liverpool — all the North's top young players will be on view.'

I looked out of the window. It was pitch black, the rain lashing down. Any faint notions of going to watch the game quickly dispersed as the thought of repeating the journey I had just made from school, to return to Maine Road in the same area, was too much even for a keen lad like me to contemplate. Soon it got to 6.15 pm. I was becoming bored and restless. *Robin Hood*, which had followed *Crackerjack*, had failed to hold my attention even allowing for the fact that Patricia Driscoll was playing the part of Maid Marian.

I checked the weather again. It had stopped raining although it was still pretty bleak. I decided to go to the match. At least it wouldn't cost me anything. I didn't pay any bus fare because Ducie Avenue was near Maine Road and I told the inquisitive bus conductor I was going to night school as he inspected my 'Ducie Avenue Free Bus Pass'.

Now that I was a fully fledged amateur player with the club, a quick flash of the counterfoil of my signing-on paper ensured free admittance to any game at Maine Road. This signing-on slip was my most prized possession. Apart from the proof to any disbelieving kid that I did actually play for City, and the bonus of its passport into the ground, it also had on the back the autograph of the greatest player of the day, John Charles. The great Leeds United and Wales centre-half had been transferred to Juventus in Italy for a record fee. I found myself standing next to him at one match and I signed him for City.

* * *

Years later, after a magnificent career during which he was rightly acknowledged as one of the best players in the world, I lined up in the back four alongside John Charles, 'The Gentle Giant', in a game at Crystal Palace. The Southern All-time Greats International XI against the Northern All-time Greats International XI. No, I don't quite know how I came to be selected other than the fact that I came from the North and was actually in the XI. However, I had no intention of letting two little words like 'great' and 'international' spoil my evening as I trotted out at Selhurst Park alongside Bobby Charlton, Colin Bell, Francis Lee, Alex Stepney and, of course, 'King John' for the game against Jimmy Greaves, Malcolm MacDonald, Frank McLintock, Bob Wilson and one or two other Southern stars.

Let's just say that I have had better nights. It didn't diminish for one second, though, the thrill of playing with the great John Charles. When we slumped down on our seats in the dressing-room after the game, he looked at me kindly, smiled, squeezed my right knee with his massive left hand and in the slightly guttural Welsh tones that had never left him, even though he had left the valleys long before, he uttered the immortal words that I will never, ever forget:

"Fred, you must be the worst player I have ever played with in my life."

Yes, John Charles actually said that to me.

It was one of the proudest moments of my life. To think that John Charles, who had played with Sivori, Boniperti, Roy Paul, Ivor Allchurch, Trevor Ford, and so many other world-class players during his glittering career thinks that I am the worst of the lot. I'll gladly settle for that.

. . .

Seven o'clock, the bus slowed down at Alexandra Park and I jumped off as it went round the corner, to land in a huge puddle. I was wearing my school shoes, as well. It was pouring down again so I nipped in a shop and bought three Mars bars and took shelter in the doorway of some unsuspecting inhabitant of Moss Side; it was absolutely pelting down.

I saw an 88 bus going in the opposite direction, back home again. I ran out to try and catch it and return home and give the match a miss. I had a walk of about a mile to get to the ground and I realised I'd be like a drowned rat when I got there, but I missed the bus and dived back into the doorway and began munching on Mars bar number one.

It tasted so lovely I immediately devoured the next one and then set out for the ground feeling a little bit more able to cope with the ravages of winter. The final Mars bar was to be for half-time, but the other two had given me such energy that I thought I'd go for my hat-trick as I walked up to the steps of the players' entrance tucking into my third.

"We've been waiting for you," said the voice of George Poyser.

I hadn't realised he was a clairvoyant in his spare time, because until an hour ago I didn't even know there was a game on. I paused in mid-munch to enquire what he meant.

"One lad's cried off and we knew you'd come to watch."

He obviously knew more about me than I knew myself.

"I've no boots," I replied, two Mars bars rising in my stomach.

"We've put Colin Barlow's out for you so get down there."

Colin Barlow was the first-team regular right-winger, a real flyer. I thought if maybe I just put them on, the boots would do the job for me. I'd never played on a big ground before or under floodlights. A dozen pairs of hands were helping me to get stripped, one putting my socks on while a maroon shirt with a big white number four was being pulled over my head. The boots were a bit tight but if they were all right for Colin in the First Division they were all right for me. Pads, I had no pads. The *Manchester Evening News* was brought, folded over and torn in half. In minute type I could read: 'All the North's top young players will be on view.' 'Christ,' I thought as it was pushed down my socks.

The bell rang, off down the tunnel, team photograph as we reached the pitch, floodlights streaming down, and my mam and dad sat at home thinking, 'Fancy Fred going to Maine Road on a night like this.'

A quick roll-call of the names of my team-mates as we kicked in, a glance to the side of the goals where dad and I always stood at the scoreboard end, momentarily choked that he wasn't there, then the game started. Who are we playing again? Chris Lawler, Ian Callaghan, England internationals of the future. They meant nothing to me that night as I gave it everything I'd got. I was elated with our 2–1 victory and dashed home later that night, my feet still bleeding due to Colin's boots, to tell my parents about the greatest night of my life. I think dad was a bit disappointed that he hadn't been there, but only a mind reader like George Poyser knew that I would be playing.

ELEVEN

Foreman of the Ground Staff

THAT GAME AT MAINE ROAD BEFORE THE EYES OF THE bosses convinced them that I should be offered a spot on the ground staff and so I signed for £4 per week. As with so many more occasions in the future I found out later that all the other ground-staff lads were on £5 or £6, but I didn't care; the money was secondary to me.

I'd always been good with money, always a good saver, never spent anything I didn't have.

"If you want something, save up for it," my dad always said to me. "Never borrow. If you can't afford it, do without."

He set me a fine example regarding money. He encouraged me to put all my shillings into a little tin box with a slot in it. I was 21 before I realised it was the gas meter.

Now I was to earn my living as a footballer, my life's ambition. But first there was the problem of leaving school. They wouldn't let me, so Dad had to pay the school £20 compensation in order for me to leave. I hadn't realised that I was so valuable to them.

Eventually it was all sorted out and on 7th December 1959 my life began at Maine Road. There were no such things as apprentice professionals in those days, although when they came into being a couple of years later I had the distinction of being the first-ever apprentice professional footballer of Manchester City Football Club.

There were five of us on the ground staff at the time and because I was 'foreman of the ground staff' I was sent for first, signed, and then told to find the others for them to be converted from 'ground-staff lads' to 'apprentices'. Every other young player signed from that day was to be known as an apprentice.

I was 'foreman of the ground staff' by virtue of being the most senior, a position usually held by lads in their last year before the club decided to either sign you as a full professional or release you. Sometimes when lads came to the club from long distances on week's trials I would be asked to look after them and take them out at night and make them feel at home.

I remember looking after Dave Clements, who went on to captain and indeed manage Northern Ireland, picking up 40-odd caps during his career with Coventry and Everton.

Ironically I next met him some 15 years later when he captained the famous New York Cosmos. We played them in the mighty Giants Stadium in New Jersey, and as we tossed up in the centre circle I reminded him of his week at Manchester City. John Hurst was another, when he came over from his Blackpool home for a week. John was a very quiet boy, easy to take care of, and I think he remained that way in his long career as a star with Everton and Oldham Athletic.

The only time during my period as 'foreman of the ground staff' that I had to assert my authority came the Saturday after one particular Good Friday. The first team had played on the Good Friday and we were to be in at 9 am the following morning to clean all the boots and get the skip ready, because they were off to play away early on Saturday. This meant us ground-staff lads all had to leave home at eight, work till dinner time, then play our own game in the afternoon, arriving home about seven o'clock in the evening—eleven hours. All told, it meant a working morning, followed by a hard game, and with no food.

There was a little kitchen at Maine Road with a tiny grill and a gas ring where endless cups of coffee were supplied to the office staff, and to Fred Tilson to try to keep him awake. I suggested to Mrs Dobell, the maître d' of the ovens, that we five ground-staff lads would club together to buy a loaf and could she spare us the use of her kitchen for about 10 minutes so we could make some toast and avoid playing on an empty stomach. This was rejected out of hand.

You would have thought we had asked for a banquet. We were not asking her to do anything. We were buying the bread and toasting it ourselves, but we couldn't reason with her. There was only one course of action to take—a trip to the office of Mr Walter Griffiths, the secretary of the whole club. I marched down to his office, my steps becoming slower and slower as I neared the end of the corridor. I stepped where no ground-staff boy had ever stepped before, into the hallowed office of Mr Griffiths, and presented our case with a veiled threat of strike action if our demands were not met. He accompanied me back to the waiting Mrs Dobell, told her to 'use her loaf' and even to poach us an egg to go on top of our toast. I should think so too.

. . .

[73]

I had read in countless boys' soccer magazines over the years that a ground-staff boy did all the menial tasks: sweep the terraces, mop out the dressing-rooms, scrub the baths and toilets each day and clean the boots.

Unlike most of the lads, I quite enjoyed doing the boots and although Bert Trautmann's size 10s were a formidable task, I always did them extra well because he was my favourite. I was in awe of Bert, our world-famous blond German goalkeeper. I had marvelled at his performances between the posts for so many years, shared the pain of his broken neck during the 1956 Cup final and now I was cleaning his boots. I would have licked them if he'd asked me. For the first month I called him Mr Trautmann and didn't find it easy to call him Bert like the other boys, but really I should have had no fears because he was super to me.

Cliff Sear gained his one and only Wales cap, against England at Wembley, around this time, and I gave his boots an extra good-luck polish because he was also a grand person and I wanted him to do well.

I didn't get off to a particularly auspicious start. The first day began in exactly the same way as every other had for the previous four years because Maine Road was only two more bus stops after my school stop at the bottom of Denmark Road.

I had cottoned on years ago that if I timed it just right, I could catch the same bus as Joe Hayes on his way to training and if I used my weight properly, I could muscle a couple of the younger kids out of the way and actually sit next to him. I loved 'Little Joe' as a player—so innocent, so nice, such a great goalscorer, and he had achieved legendary status as far as I was concerned by scoring in the 1956 Cup final against Birmingham City, by latching on to Don Revie's clever back-heel and firing it across Gil Merrick's body into the net for that vital opening goal.

So I used to sit next to Joe on the bus most mornings for years, but never said a word to him. Sometimes he was with other Bolton or Golbourne-based players like Alan Kirkman or Jimmy Pennington but usually he was on his own, as indeed he was this particular morning, my first morning at Manchester City Football Club.

I had left home at precisely the same time as before, boarded the usual number 26 bus, to the 'Halfway House', just in time to jump on to the 76 and grab the seat next to Joe as the driver wended his way to Moss Side. Kids who were, until the previous Friday, my school-mates got on at various stops and as usual, as the bus reached Denmark Road, there was a mass exodus of such proportions that the only two people left on board were Manchester City's inside-right and the kid who usually got off with everyone else. Joe gave me a sideways glance, but said nothing and two stops later, I stood up to graciously allow him to get off first and then followed him down the stairs. He jumped off and so did I. He turned left and so did I. Sauntered the length of Wykeham Street. Said 'Good morning' to two ladies in high heels and fish-net stockings. I thought to myself, 'What are they doing fully made up at ten past nine in the morning?' He turned right into Maine Road and so did I. A quick glance over his shoulder as he trotted up the famous steps leading to the players' entrance confirmed the fact that I was still just a few yards behind him. Then he finally bolted down into the sanctuary of the dressing-room in one last vain attempt to shake off his stalker. But he needn't have worried, because once down those stairs, he turned right and confidently strode into the first-team dressing-room, while I nervously turned left into the arms of Jimmy Meadows, who welcomed me to the club and introduced me to my fellow ground-staff lads changing in the little referee's dressing-room.

Striker Paul Aimson and inside-forward Mike Pearson I already knew from my representative games for the county. Ken Fletcher had been the captain of Manchester Boys when I played and David Wagstaffe was also a graduate from Manchester Boys a couple of seasons previously so I felt quite at home in their company.

The first training session went fine and I simply felt that this was the place were I was always destined to be. After training, it was time to buckle down to the chores that all ground-staff lads at every club at that time had to suffer. Hosing the baths down with a cold hose-pipe wasn't a problem, in fact it could be quite satisfying at times, as some stray spray found its way into the path of somebody who had just kicked lumps out of you during the five-a-side. I could have done without sweeping out the big gyms, all that dust swirling around. Mopping out the dressing-rooms was fine, if I could just do the away team. The home team was a different proposition altogether. For a start Bert would be in there. What would I say if he spoke to me? I'd just gape at him. I could just imagine Little Joe saying:

"Have you done your homework?"

Paddy Fagan and Billy McAdams, I'd heard them talking together and couldn't make out what they were saying to each other in their Irish brogue, so I would have no chance if they were ever to speak to me. So I almost crept into the first-team dressing-room, brush in hand ready to sweep it out. I'd been at the club since Monday and I don't think that half of the players knew I was even there, although I had already been given one valuable piece of advice in how to 'skive' in training.

"Make your arms and legs go fast, it makes Jim think you are running fast," I was told.

Footballers are obviously smarter than I thought.

This was Friday, though, and the whole of the senior staff was sitting waiting in the dressing-room for news of which 11 had been selected for the first-team game the next day. I was quietly sweeping away when the dressing-room door burst open and in bounced Dave Ewing, the big raw-boned Scottish centre-half who had held City's defence together for the past few seasons.

He looked straight at me and in that rasping Scottish voice of his:

"Hey, Ginger, what's the team?"

I felt my face flush as some of the best-known footballers in England focused on me waiting for my reply. I was struggling. I thought I knew all my jobs — boots, baths, sweeping, we even had to wash five lots of kit each Monday by hand. But maybe this was only a Friday job, to go to the boss's office, find out the team and tell the senior pros. I played for time, my experience with John Thaw flashing through my mind.

"I don't think the boss has picked it yet," I stuttered, praying that I'd come up with a satisfactory answer.

Big Dave looked round at all the lads in bewilderment at my reply and roared:

"Is he bloody stupid or what?"

He turned back to me, emphatically tapping his wrist:

"Fer Christ sake, what's the bloody team?"

I couldn't get out of the dressing-room quickly enough, and as I left I heard somebody inform him:

"It's quarter to eleven, Dave."

TWELVE

Lilleshall

Part One

I WAS THOROUGHLY ENJOYING MY LIFE AS A YOUNG footballer. I thought I was playing well and as I walked up the steps to the main entrance of the ground I felt an immense feeling of pride reporting for work each day.

It was a wonderful feeling to be fit and healthy due to the training and also to be working at something you loved doing. Most players feel like this and my advice to them is to enjoy every minute because when it's over you're a long time finished.

One of the bonuses of being with a big club like City was that at the end of the season they would send all their best young players for a week's coaching to Lilleshall, where they would be coached by the country's top coaches and the then England manager, Walter Winterbottom. This was a first-class idea and it also helped you to meet, mix with and play against the best youngsters from top clubs all over the country.

Lilleshall is a large recreation centre with oak-panelled walls and long corridors, with many dormitories for the various teams to sleep in. It stands in huge acres of grounds and parklands in the little village of Newport, Shropshire, and possesses every conceivable facility. It was used as a base for the England squad when we won the World Cup in 1966 — all the preparations were done there. You breathed, ate and slept football for the whole week, and I was glad to be one of the seven boys chosen to represent the club at this prestigious gathering.

My week there was well spent. Even in those early days I was watching the coaches perform as closely as I was watching the actual sessions. I knew the value of having the luck, when you picked a player at random to assist you with your session, to choose a lad who listens and who is capable of demonstrating what you are trying to say, accurately.

In later years when I was taking my coaching badge examination I was a little put out to be told my subject was to be goalkeeping, and I was really fortunate in my choice of a lad, Keith Coates, who performed heroics for me and finished the session covered from head to toe in mud and glory while I passed my examination quite comfortably. I will always be grateful for his efforts and for my good fortune in picking him.

I am sure that this particular staff coach, who eventually went on to become manager of a top First Division club, must have had the same feeling this day when, from a group of players all eager to learn and assist, he chose me to be his guinea pig. Now, while I was a very nice, willing lad and was prepared to do virtually anything he asked me to ensure the success of his session, I wasn't prepared to allow him, staff coach or not, to make a fool of me in front of 50 of the best young players in England, just to further his own reputation. The session was to illustrate 'balance and control' and after one or two little examples where he would start with the ball perfectly under control, he then invited me to lunge in at him like a wild bull, whereupon he would neatly side-step me like a triumphant matador and dribble the ball away. One or two more little examples like this followed and I dutifully kept diving in and missing both him and the ball. I felt I was being very accommodating, the perfect foil. However, success seemed to go to his head because he then tried to top this off with:

"When I've got the ball under complete control I can do anything I want and you won't be able to stop me."

I nodded, still feeling quite calm and still prepared to be his stooge. He then confronted me perfectly balanced with one foot either side of the ball and proceeded to kneel down, goading me to come and take the ball off him. His plan then was to get to his feet quickly, side-step me, dribble the ball away and leave me looking even more stupid, which didn't appeal to me at all. He obviously misjudged my speed off the mark, for no sooner had he invited me to take the ball off him than I covered the necessary few yards and while he was kneeling behind the ball whacked it firmly and resoundingly into his bollocks. I smiled a wry smile as he was helped away groaning.

Players should only be coached on what they can do in actual matches. His attempt to ridicule me in front of the other players didn't impress the lads one bit, which was illustrated by Tommy Smith's remark when I rejoined him in the group:

"Yer should have gone over the top and squashed the bastards."

Tommy always believed in going for loose balls, even at 16 years of age.

There were two main events at Lilleshall, the five-a-side competition with all the teams competing and the big match between the staff and the best 11 players there. I knew I had absolutely no chance of being selected for this, because it was virtually an England Youth side and I realised as the week went by that there were some really great youngsters there.

I was a bit dubious about my chances in the five-a-side as well because there were seven of us and you don't need to be a mathematician to work out that two of us were going to be unlucky. As I was the most junior player there it was odds on I was going to be one of the lads to miss out. I had already resigned myself to this when Johnny Hart, who was in charge of us, came to our dormitory to announce his selection to represent Manchester City in this big competition.

As I expected, I was not in it, but included in the team was Alan Baker.

Alan Baker was a great little inside-forward who had, the previous year, been the star of the England Schoolboys team. He was a smashing lad, who, during the week, was great mates with me and the rest of the lads, and spent nearly all of his time in our dormitory. The only problem was, he played for Aston Villa!

"John, how the hell can he play for us when he plays for Aston Villa?" I steamed in. "It's not as though we are short of players, there's three of us here who would give anything to play."

John was adamant and flatly refused to change his mind. I looked hard at him. I was only young and daren't have told him what I thought of him at that moment, or I would have been on the next train home. I went back to the other two lads who had been left out, Neil Young and Roy Thurnham. They too were obviously far from happy. I told them I was going to do something about it. Along the hallowed corridors I went, up to the imposing door, and knocked quietly.

"Come in," a posh voice said.

I entered the private quarters of the now Sir Walter Winterbottom, England team manager and director of FA coaching, and enquired if it were permissible for a five-a-side team called Fred's Gang to enter the competition alongside Arsenal, Aston Villa, Manchester City, Manchester United and all the other giants. I reasoned that somewhere there must be two other unlucky lads who had not been selected for their respective clubs and would fancy playing for my team, therefore enabling them to take part in the competition. Mr Winterbottom, who was a great student of the game, a deep thinker who, tactically, was years ahead of his time in terms of coaching, looked at me kindly like the schoolteacher he used to be, chuckled, thought about it, but finally agreed. So my team was entered — now I had only to find two more players.

I went to each bedroom in turn, but most of the clubs had only brought five players with them so they were all selected for their rightful clubs.

Finally I acquired a Scottish lad, Ian Cairns from Aston Villa, and eventually came across Barry Gould, a centre-forward from Arsenal. Barry was keen to play but his enthusiasm waned a little when I told him he had to play in goal; still it was a game, so he played in goal.

We settled down in the auditorium to watch the competition start and I was immediately struck by the lack of organisation by most of the teams.

Our own team, Manchester City, including guest star Alan Baker, were unceremoniously eliminated in the first round. Before our first game I called a hurried team talk in our bedroom. In view of the fact that we were 'so inferior' I thought we stood a better chance if we had a set plan. So I instructed big Roy Thurnham to patrol our own goal area, so cutting down the number of shots poor Barry might have to save, told Neil Young to do no graft (he was delighted to hear this) but to stay right up front and to remember his shooting boots, and that Ian Cairns and I would do all the work; this, I thought, would be better than everyone chasing aimlessly around the gym as most of the other teams seemed to be doing.

In the second round we disposed comfortably of Southampton, the conquerors of the Manchester City team plus, of course, Alan Baker, and then went on through the various rounds to beat, much to Ian Cairns' delight, Aston Villa in the final, minus, of course, Alan Baker.

Throughout the competition we scored 23 goals, every one of them by Neil Young. He appreciated the hard work we had all put in, but it was a tremendous achievement on his part and it was with a feeling of great pride and self-satisfaction that I led my team, Fred's Gang, up to receive our trophy and medals from Joe Mercer, ironically manager of the defeated finalists, Aston Villa, and even more ironically the man for whom, in the future, Neil would win the FA Cup.

As we left the arena I couldn't resist a sly glance at the City lads sitting there with Johnny and, of course, Alan Baker.

Part Two

The following year we were back again, only this time I was obviously a more senior player. John was in charge of us once more and when the subject of the five-a-side competition was raised, he asked me:

"Who do you want in your team?"

Now that was a bit more like it, I like a man who learns from his mistakes. So after deciding to stick with my 'master plan' of the previous year, I plumped for Big Mike Batty to do the 'area patrol', Neil to do the same job as last year, with Ken Fletcher and I doing the donkey work. We again didn't have a keeper so we persuaded Derek Floyd to go in goal.

All the big clubs were as disorganised as before and we walked through the rounds to beat Bristol Rovers 4–1 in the final to prove the previous year's effort was not a fluke. Neil, just for a change, scored all the four goals. We managed seventeen goals all together this time round. I nicked in with three, as did Ken Fletcher, with Neil having a very subdued time by only scoring eleven— he must have been slipping.

To crown a very rewarding week I captained the Best XI team against the staff, led by Billy Wright, and received a personalised coaching book from Walter Winterbottom to mark the occasion.

See you in a couple of years, Walter, I thought, when you present me with my first England cap.

THIRTEEN

A Professional at Last –
Lying Down on the Job

MY SUCCESS AT LILLESHALL MUST HAVE REACHED THE
ears of the boss — thank you, John. The week after I returned
home, I was signed as a full-time professional on £10 per
week. My mates got £12.

No more boots to clean, only my own. Even though it was
now in order to let my former apprentice colleagues do them,
I insisted on looking after them myself.

Things were going quite well. The Youth Cup team, of
which I was the captain, was quietly progressing through the
rounds. Leeds United, with Gary Sprake, Paul Reaney,
Jimmy Greenhoff, Terry Cooper etc., were accounted for 3–1,
Neil converting a couple of my crosses for two good goals. We
nearly had a slip-up in the second round, however, when we
were two goals down to Burnley at Turf Moor. Willie Morgan
was having an inspired day on the right wing for them and we
were finding it difficult to cope. We managed to peg goals
back from Neil Young (who else?) and one from Glyn Pardoe
to equal the score. It was a tremendous game: end-to-end stuff
with neither side prepared to concede an inch.

In the dying minutes I picked up a ball and ran at the
Burnley defence. As a wall of claret and blue converged on

me, I slid on my back and managed to set Neil free with a toe-poke pass while at full stretch. From my prostrate position on the ground I watched as Neil's usually trusty left foot hammered the ball wide of the goal. Such was my disappointment that while I lay there flat out, I put my hands to my head and lay with suppressed despair that this final effort had gone without reward — not an unusual reaction in the circumstances.

Two seconds later I was back on my feet racing into position to commence battle, and indeed from the resultant goal kick it was my header which sent Glyn Pardoe free to score his second and winning goal. We all went berserk, and about 15 seconds later the final whistle signalled a fine victory. We danced back to the dressing-room; what a comeback.

We were still jubilant as we prepared to enjoy our well-earned bath. Johnny Hart was praising our never-say-die spirit when the dressing-room door burst open and in strode the vice-chairman. Albert Alexander was a tiny, sprightly old gentleman with silver hair and a piercing voice. We mortals hardly ever saw him but he seemed a nice man to me. He stood in the doorway, looked round at all the happy perspiring faces, and immediately singled me out.

"You!"

He pointed his finger at me accusingly.

"Were shattered. I've never in my life seen a Manchester City player lie down during a game before."

I'm still not sure even now if he was being serious or not.

"Forget it," said John, but I knew that would be easier said than done and I hoped he wouldn't be there for the next round against the old enemy, Manchester United at Old Trafford.

We went into this game feeling very confident — over-confident as it turned out — because we had beaten them twice in the previous month.

It was a particularly nostalgic night for me because my old school pal Bob Smith was captain of United that night, and after we tossed up in front of 15,000 people, quite a large crowd for a youth match, we stood together in the centre circle while the teams changed ends and arranged to see each other in The Plaza after the game. Ducie Avenue seemed a million miles away.

We played terrible. I had a diabolical game, got myself booked for a foul on Alan Duff, which wasn't really like me at all, and we thoroughly deserved to lose three-nil. My performance in this showpiece game was a big disappointment to me, and as I trudged away from the visitors' dressing-room past the home team's, I glanced through the little window in the door and the only thing I could see was Bob zipping up his pants and preparing himself to meet me in The Plaza. I decided to give it a miss.

. . .

The Plaza was our meeting place. Bob and I were regular visitors, both at lunch-time and some evenings. It was a dance hall on Oxford Street in Manchester. Apparently it had been quite an ordinary sort of place for a number of years, but I only remember it from when Jimmy Savile swept in and transformed it. Now it was the rendezvous for all the young people around Manchester and the idea of lunch-time musical interludes and snacks with DJs like Dave Lee Travis playing records for the admission fee of sixpence for two hours was a winner. What value and what good clean fun.

We never used to dance. Bob fancied himself as a bit of a mover but never really got the chance to prove it. We just sat listening to the music and chatting. All the City players used to go each lunch-time, but Bob was usually the only one from United.

After lunch, if I didn't go back training, four of us — Derek Panter, Paul Aimson, Bob and myself — would spend the afternoon either playing table tennis in the YMCA or going to the pictures.

Our stature as footballers gained us free admittance to either place and even though there was a sneaking thought at the back of my mind that the afternoons could be put to better use, life was idyllic and free from worry. It would all change soon enough.

FOURTEEN

Jobs for the Boys

THE CLOSE SEASON IN THOSE DAYS WAS THE TIME OF year when the stars took a break, but for the youngsters it was a chance to earn some extra money.

The club still paid us, of course, during the summer, but with almost three months off some of us looked for part-time jobs. The previous year I had helped my dad in the butcher's shop and learned the first lesson in the art of butchering: if you knock the knife off the block don't catch it.

I learned this the hard way. I was boning out a huge piece of meat on my first day. My reflexes were ultra sharp as I just managed to catch the knife, by the blade of course, before it hit the sawdusted floor. I stood there amazed at my own stupidity as it dug into my hand, blood oozing through my fingers. And it was so cold; they didn't need a deep freeze in that shop. I don't know how my dad could stand it. It certainly wasn't the life for me.

This year, though, the four of us had decided that we would get ourselves a vigorous, healthy job. We would perform outdoor tasks and return for pre-season training bronzed (or in my case red and freckly) and raring to go. Thus, we four willing hands reported for duty at 8am to Fog Lane Park, a large park in South Manchester, where I had actually played many times for Ducie Avenue, to start work as council gardeners.

I had never lifted a finger in our garden at home. I thought hydrangeas were a Scottish football team. Bob, who lived next door to Gosling's Fish Shop on Moston Lane, didn't even have a garden, neither did Paul in Landseer Street, Salford. Derek lived in a nice house in Chorlton but being the sort of lad he was, he only slept in his garden. We all volunteered for 'hedging' on our first day, thinking it might just be within our capabilities.

We were expected to trim the hedges of the whole park in one day. We managed about a hundred yards between the four of us, as we joined in a game with some kids, with the traditional coats down for goals. This became a regular daily event, developing into a series comparable with the World Cup as word soon got round the neighbourhood, and it was inevitable that we would be hauled before the boss, 'Washy', and told to buck our ideas up.

To remove us from the temptations of games of football, we were transferred to a housing estate in Hattersley, near Hyde, to mow the lawns of old people who couldn't mow them for themselves.

The old people loved having four footballers to chat to and spoiled us with coffee, sandwiches and the odd shandy. In return for their kindness, they never got their lawns mowed. Again we were summoned by Washy for another warning.

After this we should have been on weeding, but the old bandstand with a double seat across the middle provided us with an ideal head-tennis court and soon a very serious competition was in progress. Paul and I were locked in a close doubles game with Derek and Bob when I heard a rustle in the bushes. It was Washy spying on us, but it was a crucial point in the game and because he hadn't revealed himself I decided to say nothing about his presence to the others.

The game continued.

"Out!" shouted Bob, whose motto in life was 'If at first you don't succeed, cheat!'

"A mile in," said Paul.

"Definitely out," insisted Bob, desperate to win at all costs.

"Come off it, Bob."

The argument raged, one saying, 'in', the other saying 'out'.

In the end, I thought the only fair thing to do was ask a neutral. I turned to the bushes and said:

"You saw it all, Sir, was it in or was it out?"

Washy stormed out of the bushes and we were immediately back in his office for a final warning. The end was near, however, because two days later we were in the pub at lunchtime playing snooker and we simply didn't go back that day.

I don't know what got into us, because basically we were four genuine, nice, harmless lads from good families. But being footballers, we just couldn't settle into doing menial jobs. Even for three months we didn't posses the self-discipline. I left with Washy's words rattling round my head.

"None of you will ever make anything of your lives if you don't make it at football. Especially you," he said, prodding me in the chest.

So with a green card stamped with 'Never to work for the Manchester Corporation again' in my pocket, we left the employment of the Parks Department. Thank goodness I'll never have to work for a living, I thought.

FIFTEEN

Enter Miss Tucker

THE SEASON OF 1962–63 WAS THE ONE I HOPED WOULD see my big breakthrough. I had already made my debut for the reserves, but even this hadn't been straightforward. I had been selected for the 'A' team yet again when Harry Godwin rushed round to our house on the morning of the game and told me Barney McDonald (another non-wing half who had been switched to my position, blocking it even further) had gone down with 'flu during the night. I was to be his replacement for the game at Stoke.

I thought I did well in a 4–0 victory and despite receiving the usual yawn from Fred Tilson at the end of the game I was heartened by the fact that the experienced George Hannah (he actually scored the third and killer goal for Newcastle when they beat City in the Cup final), Scottish international Jackie Plenderleith and winger Ray Sambrook all made it their business to say how well they thought I'd done. I remember their expressions and I believe they really meant it.

Even so, come the following Friday, the team sheets were pinned up and mine was the only name missing. I hung about a bit after everybody had gone home, expecting Fred to give me a 'You did alright, son, but ...' sort of explanation, but nothing. I left feeling desperately disappointed, but after my bitter experience at St Helens I wasn't really too surprised because that too had been a 4–0 away win.

That Friday morning ritual with the team sheets illustrated perfectly the different direction that Neil's and my career were heading. I used to look at it to check if I was playing while Youngy used to look to see what time the coach was leaving.

I have now come to accept this sort of non-communication as a normal part of the game, but have never really been able to understand the reasoning behind it.

Shortly afterwards my night-school pal Malcolm Darlington (we enrolled together in the Moss House wood-work class where we were both very adept at making sawdust), a left-winger with a flair for goal scoring, was named in the first-team squad for the away game at Spurs. 'Debut for Darlington' was the headline in the *Evening Chronicle*. 'Darlington Plays', quoted another paper.

On arriving at White Hart Lane, all the players, including Malcolm, went to inspect the pitch. As usual, when they returned to the dressing-room all the kit was laid out, with each player's boots next to the kit he would be playing in. As all the other players began to strip, and Malcolm finally found his boots still in the skip, he began to realise he wasn't playing.

All day Friday, the evening at the hotel, Saturday morning, the game and the journey home — not a word was said to him. He lives in Northampton now, but whenever we meet the first thing I always ask him is:

"Has the Boss told you whether you're playing against Spurs yet?"

We have a good laugh about it now, but it wasn't funny

at the time and indeed he never did make that debut. Most managers are former footballers themselves, so they should know a player's feelings and insecurities and realise that they appreciate honesty more than anything else; I know I certainly did.

One manager said to me before a game:

"I'm leaving you out today, even though you played well in the last game because the winger you would be playing against this week is a real flier."

"Hang on a minute," I protested. "He's not as quick as the one I marked last week at Wrexham."

"No, I agree, but if you hadn't kept taking the ball off him you'd have got a right chasing, and we can't be that lucky two weeks on the run."

"Mmm, I see. I haven't had it explained to me like that before."

You can't get more honest than that.

· · ·

After a disastrous season, Manchester City were relegated and the season also turned into a nightmare for me, with my injury and subsequent free transfer.

So I didn't captain England while at Manchester City — but, on a lighter note, my innersoles did. Earlier in the season there had been an England friendly match played at Maine Road. Bobby Moore was complaining about his boots and asked for a pair of innersoles. None could be found, so I graciously nipped into the boot room and gave him mine from out of my own boots. I can't understand how those innersoles could play so badly the previous Saturday yet play so well for England. They must have possessed the big-match temperament.

As Bobby climbed the steps to the Royal Box a couple of years later on the greatest day in English football history, to receive the World Cup from the Queen, I wondered if he was still wearing my innersoles.

. . .

The only redeeming feature about this particularly sad period was that a little bit of romance entered my life. I used to go out at weekends with the City lads and Bob, but really only for the company and a change of environment. What I really enjoyed were our lunch-time sessions. Females were quite a way down my list of priorities, which obviously had football at the top of it and saving up for a little car a close second.

The Plaza was still the number-one haunt at lunch-time, but a little coffee bar in Lloyd Street was making quite a name for itself since the 'Under new management' sign had appeared. It was called The Oasis and it was clean and well run. They served a handsome cup of coffee and they didn't let any riff-raff in, 'a directive from the owner'.

The owner was a certain Ric Dixon, a short stocky young man who stood no messing from anybody and who soon gained himself a reputation as a hard-headed businessman. He knew exactly what he wanted and made sure nobody stopped him getting it. He ran The Oasis in a firm and businesslike manner. His attention to detail made all his customers feel comfortable because he made sure they came first.

When he introduced local pop groups to The Oasis they made the lunch-time sessions go with a swing and it became a worthy challenger to 'Jimmy Savile's Plaza'.

The Beatles played there for a fiver between them, Gary Glitter, or Paul Raven as he was then known, for half that. The Hollies were big favourites, and Freddie and the Dreamers, who were in later years to make me captain and honorary member of their football team. I played dozens of games for them and helped to raise a lot of money for various charities. Great lads. Herman's Hermits also featured — one of the group, Lek, and I had our coats pinched one lunch-time. Definitely not the Oasis image, and Mr Dixon scoured Manchester to make sure they were recovered. Freddie Starr and the Delmonts, Gerry and the Pacemakers, Billy J. Kramer, Wayne Fontana and the Mindbenders, you name them, Mr Dixon introduced them to Manchester.

It's little wonder that he went on to become one of show business's top impresarios, handling the careers of some of the world's top recording stars.

This particular lunch-time I was sitting in his establishment with Neil Young, sipping our frothy coffee, listening to The Hollies and generally surveying the scene. My eye fell upon a pretty dark-haired young thing with enormous eyes and nice legs, and I watched as she fluttered about the place. She never kept still; finally she went behind the counter of the bar and poured herself a cup of coffee. What a nerve.

"Who's the girl in blue?" I asked Neil, who by now was becoming an authority on any female in Manchester and the outlying districts between the ages of 16 and 25.

"She's the owner's sister-in-law. Her name is Judith Tucker

and she works opposite the YMCA on Peter Street in a travel agency. She used to go to Ladybarn School and she hasn't got a boyfriend," was Neil's quick synopsis. I knew he wouldn't let me down.

I watched her for a few more lunch-times and decided it was about time she made my acquaintance. I asked her to dance, definitely not one of my strong points, and then let her know that it would be quite acceptable to me if she wished to take me to the pictures. She admired my cheek and we began to go out regularly after that. The poor girl didn't know what she was letting herself in for.

"Dad, this is Fred, he's in the process of getting the sack from Manchester City, he can hardly walk due to an injury, so the prospects of him getting fixed up with a new club are remote, and apart from football he's never done a day's work in his life."

Hardly the ideal introduction to a future son-in-law, but that was about the size of it, so it was no use trying to disguise it.

Even in those early days Judith was a great support to me, and at that time I needed all the support I could get. She, along with my mam and dad, kept reassuring me:

"A club will have seen you play before your injury so don't worry, I'm sure something will turn up."

But as I went to Maine Road for the last time to collect my boots, I already felt out of place, a stranger. Nothing had turned up. The only player I saw that day was Glyn Pardoe. He wished me good luck as I walked slowly along the corridor with my boots in my hand, a feeling of emptiness in my stomach. I somehow managed a forced smile of bravado when my pal Jimmy from the main office popped his head out of the door to say goodbye.

"Of all of the lads, we were hoping that you would get another season to prove yourself," he said. "It's been heart-breaking watching you battle the way you have, but really it wasn't even a near miss."

"What do you mean?" I said.

He glanced quickly over his shoulder to make sure that nobody was watching or listening.

"Have a look at this," and he handed me my assessment from Johnny Hart to the manager.

On the slip were written three words: 'NOT—FOR—ME.' Nothing more, not, 'a good passer but ...' not, 'an excellent trainer but ...' not even, 'a lovely lad but ...' Nothing. For four years at the club and for as long as I could remember before that, I'd worked and thought about nothing else and at the very end, I was worth just three words.

Obviously at many clubs in the future, this would be reduced to two words, the second one being 'off', but at that moment I just stood and stared at that piece of paper. If I had been in Cromford Court, I would have thrown up down that grid again. It was obvious that as far as John was concerned I was not 'for him', but in my naivety I thought he would have needed to explain to the manager the reasons why. Not that Mr McDowell would have been the least bit interested. Why should he be?

So that was it. Dream over. Where do I go from here?

SIXTEEN

The Lincoln Imp

WE WERE WELL INTO THE SUMMER OF 1963 AND VERY little was moving. Especially me. My leg was healing, but slowly. It seemed that every flag on the pavement was a potential trap, as I always seemed to find the uneven one to stub my toe on as I shuffled along. I inevitably twisted on every kerbstone, setting my progress back a few days. Whenever something is sore you always manage to bang it.

I had received one or two tentative offers of trials. That dreaded word—trial. I know how Martin Bormann felt. I was a fully fledged pro now and I didn't think I should be having trials.

"They either want me or they don't," I reasoned, but in reality I wasn't in a position to argue.

My summer holiday, a long awaited sojourn to Butlins with Bob Smith, Dave Latham of United and our pal Peter Podmore (one of my assailants with John Thaw in my Ducie days), was nearly upon me and I was anxious to get my future sorted out before we four ex-Ducie boys hit the high spots of Pwllheli.

An offer of a trial at Preston North End—good club, I thought, but a trial! An offer of a trial at Chesterfield. If it's to be a trial it might as well be Preston rather than Chesterfield. An offer of a full contract with Runcorn.

"Don't think me disrespectful," I said to their manager, Jack Boothway, on the phone. "But Run who? Are they an Irish team? Thanks very much for your offer, I'll let you know."

In a couple more years I would get to know Runcorn and many more non-league teams very well, indeed they were one of the best.

An offer of a contract with Port Elizabeth in South Africa — but I didn't think I'd be able to get home for my dinner, so I declined with thanks — and finally two offers of Fourth Division football from Workington and Lincoln City, both arriving on the same day.

A quick check on the map revealed that they were both approximately the same distance from Manchester, but the name of Lincoln painted a much more promising picture for me, so I arranged to travel down there to meet the manager and have a look round.

The Workington manager, Ken Furphy, had a narrow escape that day.

As this was yet another big day for me, my dad took his second day off work in 30 years and drove me the 90-odd miles to Lincoln.

Lincoln is a lovely city. In the shadow of the cathedral perched majestically on the hill, the whole city had an old-fashioned charm. Everybody seemed to travel on bikes or on foot and the pace of things appeared quite leisurely. These were my first impressions as we had a quick tour of the city before making our way to Sincil Bank.

We arrived at the ground just before lunch-time, much to the displeasure of the manager, who had been waiting for me at the railway station. I was sitting in his cluttered little office under the stand when he stamped in, far from pleased.

"He's not bothered to turn up," I heard him say to his trainer Bill McGlen.

Before Bill had time to reply, he opened the door and entered his office. I hadn't told him I was coming by train so didn't feel an apology was necessary on my part, but instinctively I felt that I didn't like Mr Bill Anderson at all.

I should have heeded my sixth sense and left there and then to take my chance at Workington, but in those days my intuition, which over the years has been developed to a fine art, was still in its infancy and I didn't have the confidence in it that I have now. So I sat tight and waited to see what would happen next.

First of all I had to pass the scrutiny of his labrador, Sandy. This was no easy task, as he seemed under the impression that I was a bone and I felt sure he would try and bury me any minute. Unknown to me, Sandy was the most influential individual at Sincil Bank; if he liked you, you were okay. The lads firmly believed Sandy drew up the retained list at the end of the season and he was actually in one of the official team photographs one year, proudly perched on the end of the front row, smiling like Huckleberry Hound.

Sandy carefully weighed me up before turning away disdainfully and now it was Mr Anderson's turn to cast his eye over me, literally. Bill, a bachelor, was a big man, overweight, with one eye that had a mind of its own and seemed to swivel and turn whenever it felt like it. I was never quite sure whether he was talking to me or not. He was a most unlikely-looking manager.

This time, however, I knew I was on safe ground because I was the only person in the room as he said,

"You are a bit scrawny, but we'll soon build you up here. I've already spoken to your landlady and told her she must give you two pints of milk and a steak this thick every single day," holding his fingers at least two inches apart.

It sounded like star treatment to me but I still wasn't sure. The city was beautiful, the ground was in good condition, the club seemed sound, the prospects bright, trainer Bill McGlen an admirable fellow, a promise of steaks two inches thick every day, what was the problem? The nagging doubt was the manager. I left with a promise that I would 'think it over' while on holiday the following week.

I set off for the delights of North Wales with the boys in fine spirits, but still a little dubious. The problem of my leg was also worrying me. It was a few months since the injury and I hadn't run a step or kicked a ball since. Would I still be able to play or would I be cheating any team that signed me? These thoughts were in my mind as the train chugged out of Manchester Exchange Station.

Any worries I had were soon forgotten when we arrived at the camp. Pwllheli was where footballers went in those days. Florida was still a swamp, Dubai was a sand dune and Puerto Banus was a little fishing creek. We teamed up with four Swansea players, including Wales international winger Barrie Jones, two Port Vale players—Terry Alcock, later to play for many years for Blackpool and Portland Timbers, and Micky Porter—plus two Tranmere Rovers lads, Dave Roberts and Dave Russell, and we had a great week.

It was at the height of the revelry that Bill Anderson played his trump card. He had learned a trick or two in his 19 years as a manager, one of which was that a player's weak spot is his ego.

We were all quietly sunbathing, planning our onslaught for the evening when the Tannoy system rang out loud and clear:

"Will Mr Fred Eyre please report to the main reception."

"This must be important," I said as Bob and I galloped there.

I was gasping when I got there, I was so much out of condition, and breathlessly took the phone which was being offered to me by a beaming Redcoat.

"Have you made your mind up yet?"

It was Bill Anderson.

"Well, not really," I stalled.

"I'll tell you what I'll do, I'll send the forms all filled in just requiring your signature by special delivery, then if you decide, simply sign them and send them back, and remember I've told your landlady—two inches thick."

Sure enough, the very next day the forms arrived and I called a board meeting of all the Swansea lads. In consultation with a think-tank comprised of members of Tranmere Rovers, Port Vale, Manchester United and Old Mostonians (Pete Podmore's team), it was unanimously decided that Bill obviously wanted me so desperately that it would be very ungracious of me to deprive him of my talents.

So on the third of July 1963 at 12.40pm at Butlins Holiday Camp in Pwllheli, North Wales, in chalet number EB17 to be precise, I signed for Lincoln City. I became an Imp.

It was an ironic place to sign. I went from one holiday camp to another.

SEVENTEEN

Welcome to the Real World

PREPARATIONS FOR LEAVING HOME WERE ALMOST complete. I'd packed my cases but there was just one little thing I needed to do before I left. I wanted to treat myself to a scrapbook. I had always craved a proper news cutting book but had never got round to buying one, maybe because I didn't have any press cuttings to stick in it. Now, with a bit more publicity imminent, I decided to splash out and buy one.

"You'll get one at any commercial stationers'," I was told.

So I journeyed into town, bid a hero's farewell to The Plaza and Oasis and set about finding a 'commercial stationer's'. I tried four such emporiums without success and had just about given up when I stumbled across a tiny stationer's shop on the corner of Booth Street as I cut through towards Spring Gardens to get my bus in Piccadilly.

I didn't hold out much hope as I went down the few narrow stairs into the basement shop, but I was in luck.

"Thank you," I said as the assistant put my purchase in a bag. "You are the only shop in Manchester with scrapbooks."

When I bought this very shop just a few years later, I made sure we were never out of stock of news cutting books.

"Look after your money," were my mother's tearful instructions as I left home to catch the train to Lincoln this sunny Wednesday lunch-time. A new life lay ahead. I was upset to see my mother so distressed at the departure of her only child but there was nothing I could do. I had to prove Manchester City wrong and I had to start again somewhere.

'Look after your money,' I said to myself and chuckled at my mam's fussiness as I sat on the train. There's no danger that I won't look after it, I thought. I'd drawn every penny I had in the world out of the bank and I tapped my inside pocket to make sure my wallet was safe.

'Nearly there,' I thought. 'Another half an hour to go, I'll nip down to the toilet and spruce myself up in case there's a civic reception.'

Must look my best. A quick wash, a comb of the locks — where's my comb? In my wallet, ah yes.

"Handsome brute."

Back to my seat to complete the journey.

"Lincoln," came the guard's loud voice.

I'd better get my ticket. It's in my wallet.

Never have I felt a sensation like that as I reached into my inside pocket. Empty. My God. Away from home with not a penny to my name.

I raced back down the corridor to the little toilet, threw open the door and there it was, lying there in all its glory. I staggered against the side of the cubicle as my legs actually wobbled with the relief. Thank goodness there were no people on board that day with weak bladders.

I grabbed my precious wallet, stuffed all the money into my back pocket, emptied the rest of its contents into my jacket pocket, and promptly threw the wallet away. I have never used one since. I don't intend to experience that feeling ever again.

. . .

By the time I'd trekked to the ground from the station with my cases, my arms felt as long as King Kong's, and I was looking forward to the two-inch-thick steak that I'd been promised.

Three other 'big' signings had already arrived when I trooped into Bill Anderson's office. He immediately sent for trainer Bill McGlen. Bill was a trainer in the old mould — big old-fashioned football boots, with his trousers tucked into his stockings, and wearing an old maroon tracksuit top with a muffler. He was a Geordie who had played wing-half for Manchester United. I'd seen him play at Old Trafford and later for Oldham Athletic before coming to 'The Imps' to work for Bill Anderson. He was a super, honest, hard-working man who loved the game.

"This is our new signing, Ted Eyre." Mr Anderson introduced me to Bill.

"Pleased to meet you, Ted, son," said Bill in his Geordie accent.

"Actually it's Fred — Fred Eyre," I quickly corrected, a feeling of foreboding spreading through my body.

He looked unsuccessfully around his cluttered desk for an ashtray to knock the ash off his cigar. Bill McGlen obligingly offered his cupped hand for the manager to deposit his ash, and I watched in disbelief as Mr Anderson promptly responded to this gesture by grinding the burning cigar stub into the palm of Bill's hand, while Bill bravely stood there gritting his teeth.

"Take him round the town and try to find him somewhere to live."

He dismissed us both with a flick of his podgy hand without averting the gaze in his one eye from the desk. I never could see eye to eye with Bill, right from the start.

I dutifully picked up my cases and followed Bill out into the streets of Lincoln to traipse round in an attempt to find a roof over my head.

I was a little perplexed. The manager had, he said, already organised two pints of milk a day and a two-inch-thick steak with my landlady, so what was I doing being hawked around Lincoln like this? I tackled Bill about it, one of the few tackles I managed to get in at Lincoln, and said to him:

"Bill, what's going on, what about mi' steak?"

"Mi' steak, son?" he said. "It might well be the biggest mistake you'll ever make coming here."

How right he was.

EIGHTEEN

Rescued by Mr & Mrs Foley

THANKFULLY SOMEBODY TOOK PITY ON THIS POOR wretch and offered me a home, actually double pity because she also took in one of the other signings, Bobby Murray, a former Scotland schoolboy international who had just been released from West Bromwich Albion. Mr and Mrs Foley were kindness itself to me and I settled in immediately in their terraced house, number 17 Pennell Street.

The house was situated in one of the many terraces that surrounded the ground, with an outside toilet and a garden leading down to the river.

Jim Foley was a grand man. He looked to be getting on a bit even then, but I never knew his actual age because he had such a young mind. We were both on the same wavelength and enjoyed a good laugh together.

I wondered if his experiences in the war had aged him. He had been in the Air Force and loved to regale me with stories of how he helped Churchill win the war. Whenever there was a flash of the great man on TV I would always shout to him:

"Here's your mate Winnie on the telly," and he would say that he looked just the same; he hadn't changed from their days in action together.

When Churchill appeared on TV showing his famous two-finger sign to the world I would get Jim going by saying,

"Look, two fingers. It's his way of telling everybody that he didn't do it all by himself, that there were two of you involved but you're just too modest to boast about it."

Jim now worked at Scampton, the Air Force base in Lincolnshire. He was also the Littlewoods pools collector for the camp, and because Jim couldn't drive I took him round the camp every Friday night to collect the pools money.

We would start about seven o'clock and sing all the old songs together until we returned home about nine o'clock. Our favourite was 'Swanee' and I sang the song while he harmonised in his thick scouse accent. In fact, we were in full song the night President Kennedy was shot. When we heard the sad news it was one of the few nights we completed the journey in silence.

All the while we were teaching his wife Jenny to drive, but inexplicably she kept failing her test. Jim would, after each failure, criticise the examiner.

"My Aunt Kate had more idea than him," was one of his favourite expressions, and it's one I still use to this day.

On the day of Jenny's latest attempt Jim was supremely confident that she would pass at last. He arrived home at tea-time with an expectant look on his face.

"Well?" he said.

"Failed," said Jenny miserably, and I literally rolled off the settee with mirth as Jim ceremoniously took off his old trilby, threw it onto the lounge floor in disgust, and proceeded to jump up and down on it with pent-up rage, before finishing with a shot Bobby Charlton would have been proud of, propelling the poor hat into the fire.

Good old Jim.

His wife Jenny was a kind person who not only looked after lame young footballers but also did a lot of charity work. She was a good cook who used to give us breakfasts of such proportions that I had to ask her for just a piece of toast because I was finding it hard to train after such a feast. Her cooking was always first class but the same cannot be said of Jim's. He deputised one day and absent-mindedly made me a cup of coffee with gravy powder instead of Nescafé. Aagh Bisto.

She was much younger than Jim and he was very proud of her, but the light of his life was his son Michael who was about seven or eight. He looked upon me as an elder brother and I used to play Cluedo and Monopoly with him for nights on end during the long winter evenings in front of the fire.

He always managed to beat me at Monopoly but, as he became one of the country's top financial experts, running the finances of one of Britain's largest companies in Geneva, I now realise I really I had no chance.

I spent one Christmas in the Foley household. Bob Murray had long since departed due to a slight altercation with Jim one evening, and on Christmas Eve Michael was safely tucked up in bed as we slowly and quietly crept up the stairs loaded up with Michael's Christmas presents.

"Ssh, follow me," said Jim, who was a bit dodgy on his pins at the best of times, his carpet-slippered feet slithering across the lino.

"Be as quiet as you can," he warned as he eased open the bedroom door to reveal Michael's angelic face in a state of slumber.

"Not a sound," he said as he juggled with his arms full of presents.

Crash. The bang and the rustle of paper nearly woke the street as I looked down at Jim, lying flat out on the bedroom floor, presents scattered everywhere. Jim had tripped over the wire from the electric blanket.

"Father Christmas asked me to give you this, Michael," he said from his outstretched position as he handed a bemused Michael the only Christmas present he had left in his hand. I slid down the wall, convulsed again. Not many people could make me laugh like Jim.

So it was these good people who took me in and I stayed with them the whole time I was in Lincoln. I trained during the day and in the early evening I nipped down to the ground after the manager had gone home, to dip my leg into a wax bath they had there. It seemed to help. You keep dipping it in and out of the red-hot wax until after about an hour your leg is like a giant candle, then you sit and hope something good is happening inside.

Some evenings I borrowed Jenny's car, which was stuck outside all day because neither of them could drive, and I would drive to the coast, Skegness or Sutton-on-Sea, and paddle for hours in the freezing sea in the hope that the briny would help my leg to heal.

After a few weeks of this it began to feel stronger and I was quite looking forward to the first game of the season. Unfortunately Bob Murray had broken his toe, so it was his turn to feel sorry for himself as he now had his leg encased in plaster.

I liked Bob. We got on well together and he revelled in his reputation as a tight Scotsman. The usual thing had happened—I signed for £14 per week, he was on £18, and after he had paid Mrs Foley his plan was that he would discipline himself to live for the week on whatever he had left in shillings and pence from his wages. All the pounds would go into the bank. I don't know where he is today but I'll bet he's a millionaire.

The night before my all-important first game, Bob's girlfriend, Heather, arrived from West Bromwich to see him. There wasn't another spare bed so Bob with his plastered leg moved into my bed and gallantly gave Heather his. I spent the whole night dodging his leg as he struggled for comfort and was feeling far from refreshed for the big kick-off next day against Grimsby. I had to gently ease my way through my first game for six months.

· · ·

The season moved along slowly and I could tell I was getting nowhere fast. In this time I received two pieces of advice from Bill McGlen.

"When you get older, son, the penny will drop," he told me.

I didn't comprehend, but he has turned out to be right. As I got older I saw the whole picture crystal clear, the bad coaches and managers, how to work around them rather than work against them. On the field, I would see moves three or four seconds before everybody else. The penny did drop eventually, but too late for me. The real secret is for it to drop early.

The other piece of advice was more direct and to the point.

"Why don't you pack it in, go home, get yourself a job and play part time?"

Pack in? Never. Throw in the towel? No chance.

Bill was right, of course, but I intended to heed the advice of my pal at the club, Ken Bracewell, a very experienced full-back from Burnley. Ken used to go out of his way to look after me and had always told me to stay in the game for as long as I could.

"When the dressing-room door closes for me, the factory door opens," he said. "Make sure it isn't the same for you."

NINETEEN

All Change at Crewe

THE SEASON SPLUTTERED ON. ABOUT HALFWAY through, my leg conked out again, though it wasn't as serious as before. I was back in action after 14 weeks and managed a few games before the end of the season, but another free transfer was a certainty as the season drew to its close.

Such was the inevitability of the situation that when Jim crept into my bedroom one morning and solemnly handed me a registered letter with 'Lincoln City Football Club' printed on the front, I drowsily took it from him, pushed it under my pillow and went back to sleep. It was actually a relief to be released.

My situation looked even bleaker than the previous year as I bade farewell to Mr and Mrs Foley and young Michael, who had not been able sleep the previous night because he was so upset at my impending departure. Three hours later I was back home. Things hadn't gone according to plan, but I had a few good memories and my new scrapbook had quite a few cuttings stuck in.

'Will Lincoln be at full strength today or will Eyre play?'

That made good reading while I was having my breakfast.

'The manager has switched Eyre from right-half to left-half to make room for the return of Murray; it makes no difference to the two-footed Eyre, who can play equally badly on either side.'

They just don't write them like that any more.

. . .

"Well, where do I go from here?" I said pensively to my dad.

He suggested writing to a couple of clubs asking for a trial. Bloody trial, I hated the very sound of the word, but I was certain that nobody would come in for me and I was right.

Then, from out of nowhere, came the offer of a trial period with Huddersfield Town. That would do me nicely, Second Division, a step up of two divisions and I could still live at home.

I trained on my own throughout the summer and reported to Leeds Road feeling in tip-top condition. I did well from the start, with promising lads like Frank Worthington, Chris Catlin and Derek Parkin. They were fine young players and I enjoyed linking up with them in training, but after five weeks at Huddersfield the 'old war wound' let me down again. I simply could not kick the ball without severe pain and I was forced to report to physiotherapist Roy Goodall, who treated me for a fortnight and then put a report in to the manager, Eddie Boot, who sent for me later in the day.

"I'm sorry, but we'll have to pay you up, son. Our advice to you is to quit the game for a year, give your leg a chance to get better and if you want to come back in a year you are more than welcome, because we feel you do have something to offer."

Eddie Boot was a gentleman, and in my heart I had a feeling he was right, but a year. The thought was unbearable. I said goodbye to trainer Ian Greaves but didn't have the heart to face the lads. I nipped into the dressing-room to get my gear (have boots, will travel). The only person there was Derek Parkin, who went on to enjoy a long career at Wolves.

"See you tomorrow, Fred," he said through the mirror as he combed his hair.

"Er, yes, see you, Derek," I lied, and I was off.

Struggling again.

I was at a desperately low ebb now. A respectable club had officially written me off; if I had been a horse they would probably have shot me.

· · · ·

It was Friday evening at Clough Top Road. Judith had come for tea and we had settled down to a night's television. I was wondering which game to go to watch the next day—as I was now reduced to just watching—when there was a knock on the front door. I remember I was sucking an orange as I answered it.

"The manager of Crewe Alexandra has asked me to see if you can play for their reserves tomorrow."

It was the journalist Paul Doherty, son of the great Peter, one of the finest players of all time.

"They are desperately short of players," he went on.

"They must be," I muttered, "to want a cripple to play for them."

But I agreed to play the next day at Gresty Road against Scunthorpe United.

I bandaged my leg up so much I looked like The Mummy

as I trotted down the tunnel wondering if it would stand up to the next 90 minutes.

We drew 1–1. I scored the goal and as I was about to leave and thank them for the game I was offered a contract. Only a three-month one, but I felt in my circumstances it was quite fair of them. So I changed at Crewe hoping for a change of fortune.

I was able to travel each day by train and my travelling companions taught me a lot and helped me regain my confidence, which had taken a battering in the last couple of seasons. Billy Haydock, Peter Leigh, Norman Bodell and Dave Whelan were all hardened pros of varying personalities and temperaments, and I learned more about life, travelling for three months with them, than I had in the rest of my life up to then.

Peter Leigh was an ex-City player who went on to play a record number of games for Crewe. He was a thoroughly nice person and I respected him a great deal. He was bright enough to think ahead to the days when he would quit football and had his own window-cleaning round in the afternoons.

Billy Haydock, also an ex-City player whom I knew from my days at Maine Road, possessed an ability to find a person's Achilles heel and play on it mercilessly. As the youngest member I was an obvious target and sometimes he really hammered me, but I didn't mind and it definitely helped me to cope.

Dave Whelan was a full-back who had tragically broken his leg in the 1960 FA Cup final playing for Blackburn Rovers, a game I was at. Since then he'd been transferred to Crewe and bought himself a little shop with his savings. Shrewd bloke, I thought. It was exactly what I intended to do. As the years rolled by, his shops became an empire of supermarkets and he eventually sold out his chain of stores, which made him a millionaire. He then reinvested his money in sports and leisurewear, and his JJB Sports empire has earned him many more millions. I didn't see him again until many years later when I pulled up next to him in his Rolls Royce at the traffic lights. I waved to him and he waved back like the Duke of Edinburgh, but I didn't feel too bad as I purred away in my own brand-new Rolls.

Not bad for a couple of scrubbers from Crewe.

Finally there was Norman Bodell, who although older than me was my special pal. He took me under his wing and really looked after me. He was a handsome bachelor who seemed to come to the station from a different direction every morning with eyes like 'piss holes in the snow' and used to stroll through training. He became one of the best coaches in the country at Blackburn and Birmingham City — by making sure players didn't train the way he used to.

These, then, were Crewe's best players and my travelling companions. Although at the time Crewe were on the crest of a slump I still found it difficult to break into the team, but thankfully my leg was standing up to the strain and was never to trouble me again. I could kick a ball beautifully and accurately now, long distance or short, which was especially good news, as I couldn't do that before I was injured.

It was while I was at Gresty Road that I began to see the light. Within a year I had gone from a First Division club to two Fourth Division clubs and I could just picture myself drifting around the teams in the lower divisions until the day came for me to hang up my boots with nothing to my name and no career to fall back on. Maybe I was becoming more mature and responsible, because I found the prospect quite frightening.

After one particularly bad result we were told to report back for extra training in the afternoon and I arrived back in Manchester at the unearthly hour of 4.30pm. As the train pulled in, Norman rushed me along the platform.

"Come on, let's hurry up before we get caught up with the ants."

This was his rather unflattering description of the normal, everyday, hardworking people who were all rushing home from work for their tea.

Only a matter of weeks later I was desperately trying to become 'an ant' myself and finding that it wasn't such an easy club to join.

My short contract was due to end the next day. My leg felt great and I'd scored a lot of goals for the reserves. The manager, Jim McGuigan, called the entire playing staff into the boardroom and announced that as from that day he was the new manager of Grimsby Town.

Great. One day to go on my contract and no manager to offer me a new one. The reserve-team manager, Ernie Tagg, the local milkman, was put in charge of the club and as he didn't know whether he would be manager for a day or a year, he couldn't, or wouldn't, offer me a new contract.

As far as I was concerned that was definitely it. I'd had enough sickeners to last me a lifetime. I would now sign for a non-league club and sort out my future life with a steady job.

But that was not as easy as it sounds.

TWENTY

A Hard Job
Getting a Job

SORTING OUT THE FOOTBALL SIDE OF MY PROPOSED new life was not too difficult.

When you are coming from a Football League club there are no shortages of offers, and my advice to any player making this move is to make sure you get the best wage you can because after that every move you make the money drops a little bit.

I was quite impressed by Buxton Football Club. Mr Wheatcroft, the chairman, was a very nice chap who used to sit at the table next to me and the City lads while we had our lunch at the UCP on Oxford Street. He always said:

"Anytime you decide to go part time make sure you let us know before anyone else."

The ground up in the hills was well kept and I was looking forward to playing non-league football. So, at the age of 20, I turned my back on professional football and signed for Buxton, who were managed by ex-Sheffield Wednesday full-back Norman Curtis. He played full-back as well as managing the club and I had the thankless job of playing in front of him and doing his running, because he must have been about 40 even then.

This class of football is completely different from league football. Obviously the rules are the same, but in those days very little else was, and it was here that my soccer education really began. It is of a much higher standard than people think; less finesse maybe, but much more physical and competitive than the Football League. Many a seasoned pro has dropped into non-league football expecting a cushy number only to receive a rude awakening, because while he was trying clever tricks on the ball, he invariably ended up being dumped unceremoniously on the seat of his pants by a burly defender who cared nothing for past reputations.

I was not a hard, physical player, but I soon learnt to look after myself. I had to, or get crushed. In fact, I came off after one game with a bruised and lacerated leg in need of a few stitches. I never did find out find out who it belonged to.

One of the coaches who helped to toughen me up in non-league was Alan Ball Senior who I played for at Oswestry Town. He used to bring his famous son to some of the local games. After one game at New Brighton I was driving home when my car broke down in the Mersey Tunnel. Alan and his son were in the car behind me and wanted to tow me out, but I refused. I didn't want people saying I'd been dragged out of the Mersey Tunnel by the Balls.

Another feature of non-league football is the quick turnover of players, and in the next few years I was to prove a prime example of this as I sampled the delights of another 16 clubs until I finally hung up my boots 15 years later. Some were good, some not so good, some downright diabolical, but each one of them was invaluable to my experience. In all, I played under 29 managers and an incredible 82 coaches who supervised me for over 1,000 games. I played 43 games in 18 countries around the world including Jamaica, Haiti, Barbados, Trinidad, Canada and the United States, and I was also a member of the only British team to have played in Cuba.

· · ·

At the moment I was prepared to give my best for Buxton in the Cheshire League, phase one of Fred Eyre's new life. Phase two should be no problem because there was a whole world out there waiting to give me a job.

"I'm going to get a job in the morning," I stated in a matter-of-fact manner to my dad one Sunday evening as we settled down to listen to *Sing Something Simple* on the radio with full stomachs after our Sunday tea; the ham had been first class this week, I'd got to the shop early.

"Oh really, what as?" enquired my dad. Which was quite a reasonable question to ask.

"Anything really, I'll find a few and pick the best," I replied.

I set off for town in my Morris 1000. It was a beautiful black car and I even remember the number plate, JEN269. Funny how you always remember the number plate of your first car.

I was to meet Bob, Paul Aimson and Derek Panter, who were to be my advisers. They were going to help me decide which of the many offers I was sure to receive would suit my talents best.

We decided to attack the big firms first.

"May we see your personnel manager, please," Bob requested as a forbidding dragon of a woman appeared from behind a partition to answer the little brass bell that each of us couldn't resist the urge to clang.

"One ring would have sufficed," she said haughtily. "Do you all want a job?"

"No," replied Bob, my spokesman for the occasion, "just Mr Eyre here," pointing to me as I straightened my tie in readiness to accept the offer.

"And what do you do?" she asked.

"Er, anything," I replied.

"Well, what have you been doing up to now?"

"A footballer," I said proudly.

"We don't need any of them," she said sarcastically. "What qualifications have you got?"

"He takes a great corner," Derek volunteered.

"And he's very good on free kicks," added Paul.

"I mean academically. How many GCEs or City and Guilds, anything? Milk bottle tops, Weetabix cards, anything at all?"

I shook my head.

"You've no chance of getting a job here," she said. "Or anywhere else by the sound of it. You should try the building sites."

"Don't be put off by that old bag," Bob reassured me, as we proceeded to knock on the door of at least a dozen more companies around town with the same result and same advice. Try a building site.

Six days and maybe thirty refusals later it began to dawn on me that I simply didn't have anything to offer.

I tried the biscuit works in Crumpsall, later immortalised by Mike Harding, whose early life was spent overlooking them. My mother, when money was a bit tight, worked there, four evenings a week for 28 bob. I was hoping to get more than that, but I didn't even have the qualifications to pick biscuits off a conveyor belt and they turned me down. They must be crackers!

We were now trying the outlying areas of Manchester and still getting knock-backs. My pals—and this is when you know what real pals are—were getting as dispirited as me.

Days turned into weeks and still nothing. Eventually we did as everybody had suggested and went to a building site, and I presented myself, all ten stone four of me, to the foreman's office.

"Plenty of jobs available here as a hod carrier." he said. "Do you think you are up to the work?"

He eyed my frame doubtfully.

"Yes, I think so," I said. "Give me a trial run if you like. I'll just go and hang my coat in that hut over there."

"That's not a hut, that's your hod," he said.

Phew. Even though I was desperate, there was no chance I could lift that.

I tried the cigarette factory where my Auntie Sylvia and Uncle Arthur worked. Nothing. What a drag.

I tried a plumber's merchants, again nothing doing. Keep plugging away. A big bakery in Trafford Park was next.

"We'll put you on our waiting list." A small crumb of comfort.

Maybe Washy would give me another chance in the parks. No, things were not quite that bad yet. Bad, but not that bad.

I thought I'd cracked it the next day as the lads pushed me into the wallpaper factory in Blackley Village and I asked to see whoever was in charge.

He strode out of his office and before I had chance to say anything he said:

"Aren't you Fred Eyre?"

"Yes," I said.

"Ex-Manchester City?"

"Yes."

"You used to go to Ducie Avenue with Bob Smith, didn't you?"

"Yes, he's downstairs," I said, warming to the man.

I brought Bob up to join in this heartening conversation.

"Did you know Mark Sidebottom at Ducie?" he went on.

"Course we do. Old Sidearse is a great pal of ours," we chorused.

His face changed to a scowl as he growled back at us,

"Well, I'm his father, Mr Sidearse. No vacancies here. Sorry."

Back to the streets.

I was really struggling. My parents were fine about letting me stay at home but I felt I was contributing nothing towards my upkeep, as I was relying on my Buxton wages to live on. I absolutely refused to go on the dole.

People who thought they were trying to help me by suggesting I go down to the Labour Exchange in Aytoun Street were really taken aback when I turned on them angrily and told them what I thought of their idea. I was being unfair but it was one thing I got really annoyed about.

"The day will never dawn when Fred Eyre goes on the

dole," I remember telling one unfortunate individual, but I must admit I was wobbling a bit.

I almost succumbed one day, when I was on my own and didn't have the support of my loyal pals. I went down to Aytoun Street, opened the door, and the smell of stale cigarettes nearly knocked my head off. I walked in about three yards, stared at the bloke behind the counter who was sorting out the jobs in his moth-eaten suit, with his unshaven face, his frayed cuffs and dirty collar, then glanced at my reflection in the glass door; immaculate, in my best suit, beautiful clean white shirt and tie, razor-creased trousers and spotless shining shoes, and thought, 'He's got a job and I haven't.' I turned on my heel and left. I was on the premises for about a minute and a half.

'I'll never set foot in there again,' I vowed. 'There's got to be something for me out there somewhere.'

.   .   .

In the evenings Bob and I decided to take the FA coaching course under the guidance of Harold Hassall, the former Bolton Wanderers and England inside-forward who had played in the famous 'Matthews' Cup final of 1953.

Even though it was early days, I felt instinctively at home in a tracksuit, confident in front of a group of boys, and I was dealing with my favourite subject: football. I hadn't succeeded in the game to a great degree myself, but it didn't mean I couldn't teach other people how to play it. I thoroughly enjoyed the course and was not in the least surprised when, at the age of 20, I passed my badge with ease.

This meant that I could now go out into the world and be paid for coaching groups, teams, or anybody who wanted me to teach them.

Looking back, it was an impressive squad of would-be coaches who attended this course every week. My pal Bob went on to become the manager of Bury, Port Vale and Swindon Town. At one time he was the youngest manager in the Football League. Wilf Tranter from Manchester United became Bob's assistant at Swindon. Billy Urmson became a respected coach at Oldham Athletic for many years. Eamon Dunphy went on to represent his country, Eire, many times in the future and I remained in the game for the next 40 years, so I think Harold Hassall can congratulate himself on a job well done.

I know I left the course with a feeling that I had something to offer in this direction, but my main priority at the moment was to find some form of employment. I was meeting Bob for my daily onslaught on unsuspecting companies. I had tried every single day, and hardly any escaped my attention; at this rate I would soon have exhausted them all.

On the way, I met my former City colleague Peter Dobing in Albert Square. Peter was an expensive signing for City from Blackburn Rovers, a fabulous inside-forward who eventually moved to Stoke City to continue his career.

"How's things?" he said.

"Not bad. I'm going to start looking for a job next week," I told him, in my mind thinking of all the refusals I had already had.

"You'll have no problem," he said as he waved cheerio. "Not with your personality."

"If only you knew," I thought.

I needed to buy a birthday card that day, so I suggested to Bob that I do this first before tackling the chore of job hunting. We could have chosen anywhere to make my purchase, but Alan Wardle, a full-back at Manchester United, worked part time in a stationer's shop in the afternoons, so I thought I might as well patronise his establishment and have a chat with him at the same time. So we cut through to St Peter's Square and into Caldwell's to the card department on the first floor. A Manchester City supporter, Mr Chris Muir, who was eventually to become a director of the club, owned the shop. I was selecting my card as he strolled over to say hello. We had a brief chat about City and I inquired if Alan was in.

"Och, he left two weeks ago," he informed me in his rich Scottish accent.

Bob immediately rolled his eyes and nodded towards Mr Muir from behind his back. I didn't really need Bob's silent hint.

"Er, have you got anybody to take his place, only I'm looking for a job," I said as Bob retreated into the distance to leave me to it.

Mr Muir looked me up and down and simply said:

"Okay then, if you don't like it after six months you can leave and if I don't like you after six months you can still leave."

I couldn't ask for anything straighter or fairer than that, so on the following Monday morning I reported to Caldwell's Stationers in St Peter's Square to become an ant.

It was a defining moment of my life.

TWENTY-ONE

A Crash Course in
Non-league Football

I HAD NEVER DONE A DAY'S WORK IN MY LIFE BEFORE then. I didn't know an invoice from a delivery note, but I had a couple of things going for me. I was grateful for the opportunity, and, as with my football, I was willing to work hard and give it everything I had. I also had a tremendous respect and admiration for the boss, Mr Muir, and I had no intention of letting him down.

Mr Muir, a proud Scotsman, was very keen on football and knowledgeable about the game, and as my employer he impressed me with his capacity for hard work. If a floor needed sweeping, he would sweep it. If some heavy furniture required humping, his jacket was off and he was getting stuck in while everybody else was still thinking about it. He also possessed a shrewd and quick-thinking business brain and it was an education to watch him in action.

His motto was 'The customer is nearly always right.' He would bend over backwards to be of service but if ever a customer went that bit too far and began to take liberties, he would tell them exactly what he thought, fair and straight to the point. He was a great man to have as my boss.

I carried his motto with me as I moved into business on my own.

There was so much to learn: weights of paper, sizes of paper, sizes of envelopes, rulings of books. When somebody asked for the A4 I told him I thought it ran from Bristol to London.

I relished the challenge and set about learning the trade from the word go. I loved serving in the shop, dealing with people and handling the accounts. There is something about a stationer's shop that brings out the best in people. So many different things, little novelties that people can just come in and have a rummage round and always find something they need.

Caldwell's was one of the best. In fact, I thought it was the best, and I was improving every day. My mates would come in for a chat and be amazed that I could actually serve people confidently and correctly with all these strange things and even give correct change.

I had the occasional pang of course, like the morning Mike Doyle bobbed in to see me and told me he was making his league debut at Cardiff that evening; the whippersnapper was on his way to a great career. Good luck to him, he was a fine young player and was in my team that fateful day when I damaged my leg against Bury, but that was now definitely a thing of the past.

"Good luck tonight, Mike," I said sincerely as he left the shop with left-back Vic Gommersall, another old pal, and I returned to my Bics and envelopes.

"Your six months are up," began Mr Muir as I walked in to see him at his request. "Have you enjoyed it here?"

"I have, actually, much more than I thought I might," I replied.

"Well, I would like to make you the manager of the place from now on. What do you think?"

I thought briefly of the other people employed at the shop that had been there much longer than me, but without hesitation accepted my promotion gratefully. I was to succeed Arthur Gee, another person who was a big help to me when I first started, who was moving to become boss of a London-based stationer's that was opening a branch in Manchester. I really had got stuck in to the job, tried my best, and at last was getting some reward.

In my football career, signing for Buxton was becoming less of a good idea as each week went by. Training in the evenings was one of the things I found difficult to get used to at first, having spent all my football life training in the mornings, but I was acclimatised to it now and it was fairly enjoyable. Unfortunately the trips over the Pennines were a hazardous task and two car crashes within six weeks convinced me that a club in a less precarious part of the North would be a much safer bet.

The week previously the car carrying a couple of my team-mates had hit a sheep and killed it as I followed in the car behind. This particular evening I was travelling alone. The weather was appalling and really I had a heaven-sent excuse for not turning up at training that night, but I had retained my professional attitude towards the game and had never missed a session. The roads were becoming more and more treacherous but as I came over the tops I could see the lights of Buxton twinkling below me. I came slowly down the hill to negotiate a right-hand bend at the bottom, but as I turned the wheel the car simply continued to go straight on. The dry-stone wall, made up of large boulders, came looming towards me as I struggled with the wheel. As I careered through the wall, a huge boulder crashed through the windscreen to land beside me on the front passenger seat.

As the car rolled over, the boulder and I bounced about inside the car together, like the last two Smarties left in the tube. The car finished up back on its wheels at the foot of the ditch, and I ended up back in the driver's seat with the boulder next to me.

I scrambled out and clambered back up the hill just in time to see a huge lorry take exactly the same route as I had and bounce down the same ditch, coming to rest about two inches away from my little car, where I had been standing not half a minute earlier. That was the end of JEN269.

Six weeks later another crash and another car written off, this time a Triumph Herald, and that was the end of my trips to Buxton, because I received an offer to join New Brighton. It would be a big mistake, but you don't know these things at the time, as I began my long and varied trek around the more sordid areas of football.

New Brighton were a former league club that years earlier had been forced to apply for re-election; this is usually a formality but this particular year they had been unlucky and were voted out. The ground was a fine one but 'The Rakers' had found life tough in non-league and it had seen better days.

From the town centre of Manchester, through the busy streets of Salford, down the East Lancs Road, through to the heart of Liverpool, through the Mersey Tunnel and another half an hour from there through Wallasey to the ground was not a journey to relish; in fact it was impossible to even contemplate. It took in those days, at the heart of the rush hour, approximately two hours. I didn't mind doing it on match days, but every Tuesday and Thursday evening as well was out of the question, which was what I told the manager when he first approached me.

"Don't worry, sign for us, just travel through on match days and train anywhere you like during the week."

I arranged to train at Ashton United with their players, and Hyde United as a second choice. Both clubs were very helpful so I duly signed on the dotted line on a Wednesday night and played for New Brighton the following Saturday. We lost 1–2 to a very strong Wigan Athletic team.

"See you Tuesday," the manager said to me after the match.

A midweek game, I thought.

"Yes, okay, who are we playing?" I replied.

"No game. Training."

"Don't forget I've arranged to train in Manchester," I reminded him.

"It doesn't state that in your contract," he said sounding more like a solicitor than the painter and decorator he was.

I realised I had made a mistake by not getting my special clause written into my contract, so now I didn't have a leg to stand on and although I hadn't been there five minutes, I knew I wasn't in for a long association with this club.

I kept it going until Christmas, when I just had to leave. I was spending all my life in my car, and even though I didn't have a club to go to I simply asked for and got my release. Another lesson learned the hard way; good job petrol was only about half a crown in those days.

I had brief spells at a couple more local Cheshire League clubs, where I served under a variety of coaches and encountered a couple of trainers during this period who were a law unto themselves. Not coaches, but sponge-men, the old-fashioned type where the 'magic sponge' ruled okay.

In one game our right-half, Arthur Trow, took a terrible knock on his ankle. It was swelling before our eyes as we gathered round him and by the time the trainer actually reached him it was an enormous size.

It looked an awful mess. His face had gone white and the pain was so severe he was actually being sick. Our trainer carefully untied his laces and gently slid off his boot, each movement being accompanied by a groan from the poor lad. Finally he managed to ease off his sock.

"Oh, Arthur," said the trainer with a look of horror on his face. "That's really bad, I can't stand that."

"Tell me the worst, what is it?" moaned Arthur.

"Your feet smell terrible."

His favourite remedy for injuries was:

"It's in the mind — run it off."

One day, a team-mate came into the treatment room on crutches while this trainer had gone for a cup of tea. He put his crutches behind the door and hopped across the room, just making it onto the treatment table. A few seconds later the trainer returned, examined the offending leg, which was eventually diagnosed as a hairline fracture, and slapped him firmly on the thigh.

"Run it off," he commanded.

The young lad looked amazed but didn't argue. He must have thought he was a miracle worker, and swung his legs off the bed and promptly collapsed in a heap on the floor.

"Christ, I'd better get you to the hospital," said our trainer. "Somebody has left a pair of crutches behind the door, that was lucky. Borrow these and go and get an X-ray."

While playing for Crewe, ironically at Lincoln, our right-winger, Andy Haddock, went on one of his jinking runs. This time he jinked smack into his beefy opponent and when he emerged his nose was spread all over his face and nothing could stop the blood flowing. Our resourceful trainer solved the problem by stuffing handfuls of grass up his nostrils.

Before long Alan Ball took me to Oswestry Town; another long journey, but this time I was becoming more experienced and had the 'training clause' inserted into the contract.

I really looked forward to playing for Alan. He had impressed me enormously whenever he had deputised for Harold Hassall on my coaching course by his sheer professionalism and knowledge of the game, and it was little wonder that his son Alan inherited these qualities from his dad.

Indeed, I remembered them both from years ago. Before I'd met him, I was marking his son in a match at Bromwich Street in his junior days with Bolton Wanderers. Young Alan was only tiny, but he could look after himself even then and Alan senior was giving him hell from the touch-line. It was all good constructive stuff and the lad certainly reaped the benefit.

I was hoping for a little bit of the same and I needed no persuasion to sign for Alan. I looked forward to Saturday's game at Ellesmere Port, because Alan had already told me I would play great because I was a great player — he told all his players this.

I should have said to myself:

"If I'm such a great player what the hell am I doing playing for Oswestry?"

But no, if Alan said I was a great player, then a great player I was.

I travelled direct to Ellesmere Port and met my team-mates for the first time an hour before the kick-off. They looked an odd sort of bunch. I knew big Jack Abbott from our days together at Crewe and I was introduced to skipper Gerry Broadhead, who clenched a huge fist under my nose and said:

"We get stuck in here."

Gerry was 'Mr Oswestry' and my wing-half partner. I could tell that he thought, even before I was stripped, that I wasn't physical enough for his team.

"This is 'Curly' Rogers, our left-winger," was my final introduction.

'Curly' Rogers — it must be a joke. You only read about that sort of a name in *The Wizard* or *The Hotspur* comics.

"Hiya, Curly," I chirped and he flashed me a friendly grin revealing a set of teeth that looked as though they belonged to somebody else.

Actually he was a nice lad, but 'Curly' Rogers — unbelievable. I never found out what his real name was.

With 15 minutes to go before the kick-off I asked Gerry:

"Where's Alan?" thinking he must make an entrance at about five to three to make more of an impact on his players.

"He doesn't come on match days," said Gerry quite matter-of-factly.

I remember my mouth falling open slightly in disbelief.

"He's the manager and he doesn't come on match days?"

I thought I'd heard a few classics in football up until then but this had the potential to beat the lot, so I eagerly followed up my line of questioning.

"How does he pick the team then?"

"I tell him who's played well," replied Gerry, who was now taking a more prominent position in my thoughts.

"And who tells him how you have played?" I went on.

"It doesn't matter, he always plays," chipped in one of the other lads.

I didn't like what I was hearing one little bit; and finally the $64,000 question.

"Why, if you don't mind me asking, is he not here on match days?"

"Because he's also manager of Nantwich Town and he can't be in two places at once, can he?"

I slumped back on my seat. We were due on the field any minute and I was trying to take it all in. I had signed for a club whose manager didn't watch us play, the captain was an automatic choice, and if you got on the wrong side of him you probably would be out of the side, plus we had 'Curly' bloody Rogers on the left wing! We only needed Roy of the Rovers at centre-forward and we would have the lot.

I had never heard of anything like Alan's position with two clubs before or since, until many years later when apparently his son went one better and seemed to be a player at Southampton, a player at Vancouver Whitecaps and manager of Blackpool all at the same time. Young Alan's son, Jimmy, is going to have to go a bit to beat that in the future if he wants to keep the family record going.

Even so, I was pleasantly surprised by our display and we beat the much stronger Ellesmere Port team one-nil. Gerry Broadhead scored the goal — he would be able to give himself a good report to Alan. One game, one win, but I wasn't too happy with the closed-shop attitude I detected there between a couple of the regular local players. They seemed to just play for themselves and during one game when they were obviously all messing about together, I let them know at the end of the game what I thought of their selfish performances.

As I got into the bath, my mate Jim McKiernan, a goal-scoring centre-forward said:

"That's you out for the next game."

And he was right too.

After the game I rang Alan Ball, who again had not been there, and inquired if I was out for good. He didn't even know I had missed that game and immediately restored me to the team for the next game and for the remainder of the season.

Eventually Alan did harness his full attention to one job and quit Nantwich to come to us, and I thoroughly enjoyed playing for him. I was secretly hoping that my chance for a return to league football had not gone, as the scouts flocked to see us, but goalkeeper Stuart Sherratt was the main target and eventually this fine keeper signed for Port Vale.

I kept plugging away, and under Alan I felt I had improved a bit more. My confidence was high as the winter weather began to bite. This did not bother me unduly, thanks to the beautiful sheepskin coat that had been a 21st birthday present from my mam and dad. They had been saving up for ages to buy it for me and I loved it. Alan loved it too and commented on its quality whenever I wore it, until one day, aware of the scouts who were regularly attending the games, I told him:

"Look, Alan, I know that you love this coat, so you sell me to a league club and I'll give it to you. You can have it."

Great coat, that was. It was still keeping me warm when I was watching games at the age of 45.

TWENTY-TWO

A Honeymoon in Shrewsbury

I WAS REALLY HAPPY WITH MY PROGRESS AT WORK. Mr Muir was becoming increasingly involved in his attempt to become a director of Manchester City. The old board of directors was holding firm against mounting pressures from press and public alike to stand down and let the younger, vigorous 'Ginger Group', of which Mr Muir was a key figure, take over and help to regain some of the past glories for the club. In addition to this he was pursuing his ambition to become a Member of Parliament by standing in one of Manchester's local elections. All of those activities meant that he was spending more and more time away from the business.

This meant greater responsibility for me. He had also taken possession of the little shop in Booth Street from where I had bought my scrapbook. A shop on Liverpool Road in Salford and one in Stretford completed the set.

I really relished the extra responsibility and dabbled in every aspect of the business. As well as serving in the shop, I helped with the buying, the accounts, and correspondence to customers and suppliers alike. I chased up overdue orders, attended to our many commercial accounts, sold office furniture and typewriters, sorted out any minor staff problems and generally enjoyed working for a living. I was extremely happy at Caldwell's, the staff was friendly and Mr Muir set a fine example at the top.

This new-found stability and worry-free existence prompted me to think that maybe Judith, who had stood by me through all my troubles, might care to join me in the matrimonial stakes. With her wages from TAP (Portuguese Airlines) and mine from Caldwell's, plus my football money, I reckoned we could manage safely and so on 21st May 1966 we were married at St Chrysostom's Church, Victoria Park.

I was up bright and early, and my best man, from Manchester City days, Derek Panter, and I were looking our best as we made our way to the church. I didn't know that while we were both actually standing at the altar, listening to the organist play the same hymn over and over again, Judith was still in bed. Her nerves had got the better of her and she was feeling too ill to stand, let alone walk down the aisle.

A few sharp words and threats from my new brother-in-law to be, Mr Dixon, got her onto her feet and after what seemed like forever she finally arrived, just as Derek was saying, "I think she's changed her mind." Much to the relief of the organist, I expect, whose fingers by this time must have been worn down to the knuckle.

Our honeymoon was to be in London, but after only one day away we had to travel back to Shrewsbury, where Oswestry were playing Shrewsbury Town in a Midlands Cup final at the picturesque Gay Meadow ground.

I received the usual ribald comments from the lads as I arrived at the ground, bits of confetti still falling occasionally out of my clothes as I prepared to take part in what was to be the most bizarre game I have ever played in.

I was marking Peter Broadbent, the ex-England and Wolverhampton Wanderers player, who had been a great player in his time and a vital player in the great Wolves team of the 1950s. Now he was nearing the end of his career but I was still looking forward to pitting my wits against him. With one minute to go the score was an amazing 4–4, the little non-league side had played its heart out to really stagger our Third Division opponents. The ball was punted out of our defence to Jim McKiernan who was on the right wing, loitering without intent. He set off down the line and I decided to take a deep breath and make one last-gasp effort to pull out the winner. While Jim was progressing down the wing past a maze of weary defenders, I was galloping down the middle as he slung over a very high cross to about the penalty spot. It was really too near the keeper but I kept running just in case.

For some reason the keeper, Alan Boswell, an experienced campaigner, completely misjudged the flight of the ball and I ran in behind him and gleefully headed the ball into the net, before turning joyfully to run the length of the stand jumping and doing cartwheels as my team mates jubilantly hung round my neck. Suddenly, silence. There wasn't any cheering anymore. We all turned to see what the problem was, just in time to see a mass of blue shirts converging on our goal. The referee had astonishingly given me offside, even though I must have run 90 yards from behind the ball, and now poor old Charlie Hughes was picking the ball out of our net. We had lost 5–4.

What a honeymoon, does nothing ever go right in football?

It was a silent honeymoon drive back home to our new semi-detached we had bought ourselves in Radcliffe, an industrial suburb between Bury and Manchester, to start our married life. I had hoped to begin our life together with a goal at Shrewsbury but as I thought more about it I decided I had a bigger goal in life to aim for. I wanted a business of my own like Mr Muir's.

TWENTY-THREE

A 'Kosher' Coach

DURING THE SUMMER MY BEST MAN, DEREK PANTER, moved from City via Torquay United to Ellesmere Port. After he had signed, the manager, Cyril Tolley, said to him:

"All I need now is a really good wing-half to complete my team, do you know one?"

Derek, being the good mate he is, said:

"No, but I know Fred Eyre."

So at his request I went to see Mr Tolley, a big, brusque schoolteacher who offered to treble my wages if I signed for Ellesmere Port. Just married, wages trebled, I didn't hesitate and I became an Ellesmere Port player. Not bad, I'd played for five non-league clubs in two seasons and there were still plenty more to go at.

Ellesmere Port had decided that this would be their big season. They would really 'push the boat out' and recruit the best players available by offering attractive wages and lucrative bonuses. I felt it was a good side and we played well at the beginning of the season, winning most of our games.

Unfortunately we were knocked out of the FA Cup in the first preliminary round. All the players felt very disappointed that we wouldn't get the chance to play Arsenal or some other big club at Wembley the following May but we didn't think it was the end of the world. We consoled ourselves with the usual excuse, 'We'll be able to concentrate on the league now.' But the committee members were far from pleased. They had other ideas. Committee members are a breed of their own; one was so lifeless it was rumoured he had been dead for a week but nobody had told him. We used to say he read the paper in bed each morning and always turned to the obituary column first. If his name wasn't in it, he'd get up. Committee members, even though they never have the nerve to say anything to the players, always manage to make their feelings known in the social club or anywhere else the spectators gather to have a drink and a moan, and usually it was from a supporter that you'd learn of any impending transfer or topic within the club.

This was the case at badly run clubs. The good clubs with strong managers invariably did things a little more professionally. Unfortunately for me, most of my non-league career was spent in the former, with a host of 'trainee corpses' at the helm.

After the latest Cup defeat, the committee members were at their best, clucking around like old hens and totally ignoring the players after the game. Despite doing our best we had committed the unforgivable crime of losing.

After much tutting and whispering we were all gathered together and informed by the manager (there was not a committee member in sight) that our wages from that moment were to be cut by 75 per cent and would we all be kind enough to raise our hands as acceptance of this 'fait accompli'. My first reaction to this outrage was one of mild amusement. Imagine the reception of the committee if we had won the Cup tie and had asked them for a 75 per cent increase in our wages. 'No chance,' would be the unanimous answer to the reduction.

I was astonished to see 10 hands being raised, mine being the only one to hang limply from my shoulder. The manager thanked the players for the 'unanimous gesture' and left the room. The players muttered their disgust under their breath but not one of them had said a single word in their own defence. I made my way over to the manager and informed him that he had conveniently overlooked the fact that I had not raised my hand in acceptance of the drastic wage cut and therefore was expecting to be paid in full at the weekend as stated in my contract.

He looked at me as though I had 'Judas' printed on my tracksuit not 'Adidas' and informed me I would be getting the reduced wage the same as everybody else. At that point I knew I had kicked my last ball for Mr Tolley.

Two more local moves provided more experience but not a lot of pleasure. At Radcliffe Borough, round the corner from our new home, we always trained in the dark. Manager Ray Gill, who still holds the record for league appearances for Chester, used to work wonders at varying our training but was obviously limited — we did our sprints on the pavement of the main thoroughfare under the light of a lamppost.

One night's training consisted of erecting a huge fence behind the goal, to stop the ball going into the big reservoir every time a shot at goal was off target. My fitness didn't improve but I now knew how to knock posts into the ground.

Eventually I arrived at Chorley and for the first time since my Buxton days I felt as though I had joined a club of some substance. The facilities were good, the ground excellent and

I felt at home the minute I drove through the gates. I was to spend a couple of good seasons at Chorley. I was entering a happy and interesting period of my life.

The moment that destined me to sign for Chorley came when I was playing for St Helens Town. My old mate from Oswestry, Jim McKiernan, had taken over as manager and asked me to sign. After all, Bert Trautmann had started his career there, so what better place?

I enjoyed playing for Jim, but he was the only professional thing about the club. During a break in the game against Chorley I was waiting to take a throw-in while our goalkeeper was having treatment from our trainer. To amuse myself I began juggling the ball from foot to foot. I hadn't had many kicks during the game so I was making up for it.

A voice in the crowd jokingly shouted to me:

"Keep that up and you will be good enough to sign for Chorley."

I responded to the joke by telling him I wouldn't mind because it looked such a good set-up.

The following week I became a Chorley player because the face in the crowd was the Chorley secretary, Jim Moscrop.

Once again I was under the charge of another clueless manager. This one preached Liverpool at us the whole time.

"Emlyn always takes up a position here, then he knocks it wide to Steve Heighway, who takes on and beats five defenders. I want you to do the same, take on and beat five defenders and then get a good cross in," he would tell our young left-winger, who a fortnight previously was playing for The Dog and Duck or some other pub in the local Sunday league.

It was absolutely ludicrous and I was relieved when he was sacked shortly afterwards, but not before he called local lad Ronnie Pickering to one side half an hour before the kick-off to give him his debut.

"Have you ever played in midfield son?" he said to Ron, who nodded enthusiastically. "Well, put number ten on and play right-back."

Coach Harry McNally and Stan Hayhurst then took over and restored some form of stability to the place. Stan, a former Tottenham Hotspur goalkeeper, was the manager, a gentleman, quiet and respected, while Harry, the extrovert, put us through our paces.

Harry's training was well thought out. He included plenty of ball work and his ideas coincided with mine. I was really enjoying my game.

I had also been offered a little coaching job in Manchester every Monday evening, coaching the top Manchester Jewish football team, Waterpark. Not exactly starting at the top but for me I couldn't have begun my coaching career in a better place.

Many of the boys ran their own successful businesses and were not used to anyone telling them what to do. They took their football seriously, but being put through their paces, punished for sloppy training, and being constantly pushed and bullied did not come naturally to them. They all had minds of their own and were used to getting their own way so a group of 20 or more of them under one roof was a pretty formidable gathering. I didn't let them intimidate me; on the contrary I ripped into them from the word go and they got thoroughly professional training and coaching whether they liked it or not. Any slackers were publicly punished with press-ups while their friends and colleagues gleefully counted them out.

In return, they gave me their utmost respect and did everything I asked of them and more. Their efforts and the improvement in their play and general standard of fitness gave me a belief in my own ability to coach and the confidence that if I could handle these lads I could handle anybody.

I coached and trained the team for three years and thoroughly enjoyed every minute of it. I knew that when the day came for me to hang up my boots I had the necessary qualifications to consider being a coach.

During this time my private life continued to prosper and I was now confident that I could handle any aspect of the stationery business. I knew Mr Muir was pleased with me, but I still hankered after a business of my own and decided it was about time I did something about it.

TWENTY-FOUR

Raindrops Keep Falling on my Head

BUSINESS WAS A LITTLE QUIET THIS PARTICULAR DAY. Mr Muir was out, so I decided to have a good look at the stock and try to calculate how much I would need to start a business of my own. I decided to do my 'stock-take' systematically by starting at the door, working my way through the shop and then into the stockrooms.

Behind the door was a very insignificant stand that housed the various typewriter ribbons. Customers never even saw it as they entered the shop, but when we were asked for a ribbon we just took one from this dispenser stand. I began my stock-take there. Fifteen seconds later my stock-check was over: I had already passed the figure I had in the bank and I hadn't even completed the count of the typewriter ribbons. I estimated Mr Muir's stock at about £20,000 and I had £150 in the bank.

I was disheartened, but not knocked out, because even though I couldn't see it, I just instinctively knew that there was some way out of this problem, some method of trading, a different approach to the job. I couldn't figure it out, but I knew it was there. I fretted over the problem every waking hour and often during the night, but couldn't come up with the answer.

It took a downpour to give me a clue as to how I could set up in business by myself, even though I had no money. A young office girl came into the shop with a list of stationery requirements, absolutely soaked to the skin from the rain.

"You should have phoned me with your list and I would have delivered the order for you," I volunteered.

She was delighted to hear this and promised to do just that in the future. It occurred to me that there must be other firms who would sooner have their secretaries remain in their offices working, earning their wages by performing more lucrative tasks than the mundane job of traipsing down to the stationer's to pick up their office requirements, especially in the pouring rain.

They could ring me and I would deliver their order to them. They would never have to leave the confines of their warm, cosy offices and I would be more than happy to get drenched if it meant I was in business on my own. I needn't carry any stock because, I reasoned, as the orders came in I would dash round to the various wholesalers and obtain the goods. So I was only buying stock that was in fact already sold. It all seemed so simple; so I decided to pursue the matter a little further. My investigations into the protocol of the trade revealed that it was frowned upon to work from home, it just wasn't the done thing, and even though I was contemplating starting right at the very bottom, I wanted to do things in the correct manner and not upset anybody. I needed some form of base, and also somewhere for my prospective customers to ring with their orders.

So every Sunday I walked around the streets of Manchester—back streets, alleys and basements, anything—

in search of a base, an address from where to start my empire. Eventually I decided upon a former women's prison in Lancaster Avenue. It was open plan and had three curving galleries of wood, cast iron and glass. It had been built in 1871 and ran from Fennel Street at one end to Todd Street, near Victoria Station, at the other, where there was a rather dubious looking nightclub. The cells had been converted into little offices and the ones which looked out onto the main thoroughfare were now little shops, each one a character of its own: a jeweller's, antique shop, sign writer, leatherwear shop, greetings cards shop, and it was among this odd assortment of traders that I decided to launch Fred Eyre Stationers onto an unsuspecting world.

I took out a lease on number 55, one of the rear-view cells on the first landing, for 15 shillings a week. It measured about 4ft x 8ft and was completely bare with no heating, but it was 'home'. I went in to see Mr Muir the next day and handed in my notice.

I left Caldwell's on the following Friday. Two days later, Monday 31st July 1967, Fred Eyre Stationers was born. No customers, no accounts, no stock, one estate car, an office for 15 bob a week, £150 in the bank, the support of my wife and parents, plenty of optimism and boundless energy.

Does anybody need more?

Mr Muir, as always, was first class. He wished me all the best and said if ever I needed help to go and see him, 'because a friend in need — is a bloody pest'.

I was on my own now, without a single customer, but if any company who traded with Caldwell's approached me I always refused. I vowed that no matter how much I might struggle

I would never, ever, approach any of Mr Muir's customers in an attempt to lure them away to trade with me and I am proud to say I never did; I was prepared to stand or fall by my own efforts.

The lifeline of my new venture was the phone. I couldn't sit by the telephone all day waiting to receive orders if I was out chasing business, so not for the first time in my life, my dear old mam came to the rescue. She agreed to stay in all day at home and answer the calls and take the orders. I would ring her from telephone boxes every hour while I was on my travels. If we had been lucky and there were one or two orders phoned in I would pick up the necessary stock from the various wholesalers and deliver it promptly to the customer.

On my business cards, which I left almost everywhere, was the name and address of my luxurious new premises, but they simply said, 'For orders ring Cheetham Hill 1200.' Nobody bothered to enquire if the phone was actually at my Lancaster Avenue premises; they all assumed it was. Nobody ever asked so I never volunteered the information. They got their orders promptly, so it didn't matter to them that my system was a little unorthodox.

My first call as a self-employed man was to my brother-in-law's business. Perhaps Jill, my wife's sister, would insist that her husband deal with me in order that her sister wouldn't finish in the workhouse. He was now very well known in show business circles with his partners Danny Betesh and Harvey Lisberg. He addressed me in his usual forthright manner.

"Yes, you can have our account, but if you let us down even

once you will be out of the door, brother-in-law or not."

I didn't expect anything else and remained their 'stationer to the stars' the whole of my business life, providing stationery for the top stars of the day: Abba, Boney M, 10CC, Barry Manilow, Dr Hook, Kate Bush and many more. If I had let them down I have no doubt he would have been true to his word and booted me out, but I had no intentions of letting him or anyone else down who gave me a chance.

Next I was sent to Ric's accountants to meet John Wright, who gave me the same instructions,

"Yes, okay, but let me down at your peril."

Suits me. They also stayed the course. Then on to George Greenall, who had been a player at City with me, but was then running his own insurance company in Handforth. Finally to another ex-City colleague, Jeff Fry, owner of a fabulous nightclub in Ashton.

All in all, a good first day.

The next day was to be my test, when I was to find out that I was the world's worst salesman.

My calls the previous day were not too difficult because I knew the four people I was going to see, but my efforts from this day forward were to be a different story altogether.

I set out to saturate Manchester. I would leave no office unturned, every single one would be canvassed by me, they would all be bowled over by my charm and personality and be queuing up to give me orders.

I hovered outside a big office block. I looked at my watch: they'll be on their coffee break, I won't go in just yet. I'll go and get a cup of coffee myself and come back later. That's no good—too near dinner-time, I'll go in after two o'clock.

Maybe I'll nip back to Lancaster Avenue and see if the post has brought me anything.

Nothing.

Back to the office block. Far too late in the day to call now. They won't want to see me at this time; I'll go in the morning. A swift drive home.

"Had a good day, love, did you get any orders?"

"Hard day, love, no orders but I'm really knackered."

I wasn't even fooling myself. I was frightened to death at the prospect of actually knocking on an office door, not knowing the reception I would get on the other side. I also knew that if I went on like this we would starve and, worse still, I would have failed in my venture. I couldn't even contemplate that.

The next morning I set off with the best of intentions, but as soon as the office door confronted me I got an attack of the wobbles. This time I could not let myself be deterred so I gritted my teeth and knocked on the big imposing oak door. It was opened by a female who looked like Brian London in drag.

"You don't want any stationery, do you?" I said.

"No," she said with a puzzled look on her face.

"Thank you very much, " I said as I retreated down the stairs.

Somehow realising I had approached the job in the wrong manner, I persisted and was pleased to report at the end of the day that I had been slung out of every office in the building. I was improving; I was at least knocking on the door.

It gave me fresh heart to start the next day. I was now moving up in the world and being ejected from all the most luxurious offices as well as the small firms. It was Thursday and I hadn't earned one single penny when I descended on a travel agency on King Street who at least had the decency to see me.

"So just give me a ring at this number," I said, pointing to my card, "if you need any stationery. It doesn't matter how little; I will deliver it personally within the hour. Thanks very much, cheerio."

"What nice people," I thought as I left the premises.

Later in the day I rang in to my mother's to see if anybody had bothered to contact us with an order. The unbelievable had happened, an order at last.

"It's from a travel agency on King Street, 'Arise and Travel'," my Mother informed me, sounding as excited as I was.

I had a quiet chuckle to myself. I knew they were good people, I thought, at Horizon Travel.

"They want a packet of paper clips," mother began.

"Yes, okay, Mam, I've got that, what else?"

"That's it," she said.

"You mean that's all they want, a packet of paper clips? It can't be."

But it was.

I put the phone down, left the kiosk and wondered at their nerve. The total order was 3d and I was expected to deliver it and invoice for it as well. The more I thought of it the more indignant I became, but then I remembered my last words to them as I left their office.

"No matter how little, I will deliver it personally within the hour."

A promise is a promise and promises must be kept.

So I arrived at the travel agency 15 minutes later with the box of paper clips.

"Thanks very much," the secretary said to me as cheerfully as before. "But before you go, the boss would like to see you in his office."

I entered the inner sanctum and was greeted by:

"I like a man who keeps his word. Now we also want three desks, three chairs and a filing cabinet. Can I have them tomorrow?"

It was like winning the pools. It was the equivalent of about the next eight weeks' wages and I assured him the furniture would be there the following day.

I was up bright and early the next day, picking up the furniture. It was no problem loading it up with the help of the warehousemen, but as I drew up outside the travel agent's on King Street it occurred to me that I was not going to be able to manage this job by myself. It wasn't the thing to ask the customer to give me a lift. Humping in the desks himself was definitely not part of the service he would be expecting. So I just stood at the kerb leaning on my car, eyeing the desks and waiting for inspiration.

"Hello, my son," came a cheery greeting in a familiar Scottish accent.

I recognised the voice immediately and I turned to be greeted by the greatest goalscorer in the world at that time, Denis Law. He looked the picture of health, his blond mane shining and his smile as broad as ever. Denis has always been great to me. When he signed for Manchester City for a record £55,000 transfer fee from Huddersfield Town, I was still a ground-staff boy at Maine Road and I used to clean his boots. He had been transferred to Torino in Italy, but had not settled down and had returned to England to link up with Manchester United. Even though our careers had taken off in the exact opposite direction to each other, whenever I saw him he was always cheery and friendly. The bigger the star the nicer the person.

Now here we were on King Street and I had the problem of my first-ever delivery for Fred Eyre Stationers, which Denis soon solved for me by taking one end of a desk as I took the other and we humped it all in together. The two young secretaries nudged each other as we brought in the last of the furniture.

"He must be doing well for himself, he's got Denis Law working for him in the afternoons."

The next day completed my first week as an entrepreneur and thanks to the furniture order it had been a profitable week. I had £129 14s 3d left of my £150 starting capital. Most of my suppliers had granted me a monthly account with the usual warning:

"Don't let me down with payment."

I knew I had no intention of doing so, but others were understandably a little wary of this youngster and I had to pay cash when I dealt with them. I held no resentment to the suppliers who refused me my much-needed credit, but I always, from that day, put them to the bottom of my list of alternative suppliers when I was ready to place big orders. I always considered the ones who helped me when I needed them most.

Despite being very pleased with my first week's trading,

I was aware in the back of my mind that it was only the furniture order that had pulled me through. I couldn't expect one of those every week.

The next week went pretty much the same way, with many, many refusals.

"Please can I see the manager?"

"Dave, there's a kid here selling stationery," he shouted over a partition.

"Tell him to piss off."

Unknown to me, that unseen smooth-talker was one of my Waterpark squad. A couple of weeks later he said after I had put them through a particularly gruelling session:

"I believe you have got your own stationery business. I use plenty, come and see me tomorrow."

He handed me a card that I stuffed into my tracksuit pocket. I made it my first call the next morning and obviously remembered the place from my previous visit. I climbed the stairs and told the same chap:

"I'm the fellow your boss told to piss off a fortnight ago. He now wants to open an account."

I still deal with them today and every time I take a further major step forward in my business, Stuart Diner always reminds me:

"You've come a long way, kid, since I threw you out of my office."

This day, however, it was just one of a dozen knock-backs as I kept battling away. Eventually, somebody ordered a typewriter and I had made a profit for the week again, but only just.

This is how it went for months, every week a struggle but

one big sale pulling me out each time, until I began to accept the fact that if you stick at it, there will always be something to pull you through. My rule when I started was, as soon as my original £150 was gone I would quit. I had no overdraft and was using my dad's principles of life in my business, 'only spend what you've got'. It got pretty near the watermark at times, but I always just managed to keep my head above water, and all the time my list of customers was growing, and every single week I managed to make a profit. This went on for the next 18 months.

During this time the boss of a big stationer's in Manchester offered to buy me out completely. I could have a nice bank balance and a top job in his company. I was flattered and tempted but stuck to my guns and said:

"No thanks."

Mam and Dad. A little before my time.

Aged three in the garden at Clough Top Road. 'Frank Swift's Jersey', a discarded Boy Scout's jumper and Mam's expertise with a needle and thread.

A home fixture for Crosslee, amongst the prefabs behind The Clough Hotel. Seven years of age.

Crosslee School, 22nd May 1951. Fourth from right, middle row.
Next left: future singing star Malcolm Roberts.

Another ambition achieved. Wearing Wilf McGuinness's number 4 shirt for
Manchester Boys. With my great friends Neil Young and Bobby Smith.
Back row (l–r): Snowball, Mostyn, Rabbitt, Trulio, Atherton (father of cricket
legend Michael), Hunter, Owens, Hobin; middle row (l–r): Nuttall, Clayton, Young,
Pearson, Eyre, Evans; front row (l–r): Cooke, Smith (V.), Smith (B.), Hewitt.

Boots by courtesy of Colin Barlow, pads by courtesy of the *Manchester Evening News* and a stomach full of Mars bars. 'All the north's top young stars will be on view.'

Lilleshall, 11th July 1961. Can you pick out Neil Young, Brian O'Neill, Tommy Smith, Barry Fry, George Graham, Lew Chatterley, Peter Simpson, Bobby Noble, George Jones, Mick Buxton, Alan Ogley, Frankie Spraggon, Eamon Dunphy . . . any more?

(Courtesy of Tommy Smith MBE)

Lapping up the training. Fourth pair from the front with my partner John Benson, behind goalkeepers Bert Trautmann and Steve Fleet, Ray Sambrook and George Hannah, and Alan Oakes and Mike Pearson.

Butlins, 3rd July 1963. A board meeting was held to decide whether Lincoln City was to be the lucky club to obtain my signature. The vote seems unanimous.

'This is Ted Eyre.' I am introduced to Bill Anderson and trainer Bill McGlen together with the other new signings. From the left: Terry Thorne, Alan Spears and Alan Morton. He got their names right.

Three legends. 'King' John Charles, 'Little' Bobby Collins and my dad on his 80th birthday.

The transformation nearly completed. My first shop in Booth Street.

Even Denis Law had to wear those smelly old brown training jumpers. He inherited the number from Dave Ewing and passed it on to Alex Harley when he left. All Scotsmen.

'I want a bit of sweat on this': A welcome to Springfield Park for Larry Lloyd from Peter Houghton, Mickey Quinn, Jeff Wright and myself.

My last game in Trinidad. My face shows I'm ready for retiring.
Bob Smith, behind me, was there at the beginning
and also at the end.

First day at Bramall Lane with (left to right) John Dungworth, Russell Slade,
Nigel Spackman, Tommo and Willie Donachie.

The Blades book their place in the FA Cup semi-final. Joy on our bench for Graham Stuart, Fred Eyre, Simon Tracey, Steve Thompson and Dean Saunders. Coventry boss Gordon Strachan is obviously not as happy as we are.

FA Cup semi-final. Sheffield United v. Newcastle United, with Tommo still trying to work out how to stop Shearer. Dalglish, McDermott and Rush in the background don't have that problem.

'Little Joe' scoring the opening goal in the FA Cup final, Wembley 1956.

'Manchester City 'Olde Boys'. Still looking good. Back row: George McDonald, John Riley, Roy Cheetham, Johnny Williamson, Fred Eyre, Shaun Goater, Tony Book, Bill McLardy, Steve Fleet, David White. Front row: Johnny Hart, Bert Lister, Paddy Fagan, Tudor Thomas, Roy Little, Ken Barnes, Hughie Murray, Peter Horridge.
(Photography by Roland Cooke)

Frank (Fred's mate).

Puskas, leading out 'The Mighty Magyars' at Wembley in 1953.
A game that changed the face of English football forever.

Manchester City Football Club, 1962. (Front row, extreme right.)

The Eyre family: daughter-in-law Claire, son Steven,
wife Judith and daughter Suzanne.

Proud Granddad with lovely granddaughters Emily and Lucy

'When Manchester City Football Club opened the doors of the magnificent city of Manchester Stadium to welcome the 2003–2004 season, Fred Eyre was back where he really belongs. As host in the clubs 'Legends Lounge' . . . where else?'

Best wishes
Bert

– Bert Trautmann, OBE

MANCHESTER CITY FOOTBALL CLUB

TEAM v.	Leicester City		TEAM v.	Everton Reserves.
DATE	14th October, 1960.		DATE	14th October, 1960.
AT Maine Road	kick-off 3 p.m.		AT Everton	kick-off 3-15

GOAL	Trautmann		GOAL	Dowd
R.B.	Betts		R.B.	McDonald
L.B.	Sear		L.B.	Leigh
R.H.B.	Barnes		R.H.B.	Cheetham
C.H.B.	Planderleith		C.H.B.	McTavish
L.H.B.	Shawcross		L.H.B.	Oakes
O.R.	Barlow		O.R.	Sambrook
I.R.	Law		I.R.	Pearson
C.	Hannah		C.	Dyson
I.L.	Hayes		I.L.	Aimson
O.L.	Colbridge		O.L.	Wagstaffe
Reserve	Ewing		Reserve	Eyre

ARRANGEMENTS   v   Leicester City.

Players to report at Maine Road at 2-15 p.m. prompt.

My first appearance in the position I was to make my own.

TWENTY-FIVE

1969 – My Year

NINETEEN SIXTY-NINE WAS TO BE THE BIG YEAR IN MY life. Mind you, it didn't get off to a flying start. I was still enjoying life at Chorley and had won a couple of medals with them. The brand-new Northern Premier League was formed with Chorley as a founder member and I played in the first-ever Northern Premier League game—a 0–0 draw with Altrincham.

I was participating in one of our Thursday night training sessions when I collided with our big keeper Ronnie Fairbrother going for a cross in a five-a-side game. It was an innocuous challenge but as our arms locked together, I felt my shoulder lift out alarmingly. Suddenly my shoulder blade was jutting out somewhere behind my left ear. The pain was worse than I could possibly have imagined. It was much worse than when I injured my leg and it was with extreme difficulty that I was escorted to hospital in Chorley. I reached the out-patients at ten to eight in the evening and at ten past eleven two doctors were still trying to wrestle the dislocated shoulder back into its socket.

Eventually there was a locking sound as it flew back into place. The three of us slumped back in our chairs, me sweating with pain, and the two of them sweating with the sheer effort of the bout, two falls or one submission. The joy I felt as it clanked back to where it belonged was indescribable. My arm was put in a sling and I was told:

"Stay off work for four weeks, then come back and have the sling taken off."

They must be joking. I couldn't afford to stay off work for four minutes let alone four weeks and the next morning, usual time, I was off on my rounds driving one-handed, steering with my right hand and just about steadying the wheel with the fingers of my left hand as I reached quickly across myself to change gear and snatch the wheel back again. Reckless, but it was either that or no food.

I had to keep working. If I stopped, the whole business ceased, because as well as the buying and selling during the day I also typed the invoices and attended to the accounts in the evenings and dealt with any correspondence.

This, in fact, went on for five years, during which time I never had one single day off, which was partly luck, as I never even got 'flu during this time, and partly design as we had no holidays either. But I loved the work, even though it was hard. Every day was like a holiday.

My first phone call of the day to my mother, the first after suffering the 'slings and wotsits of outrageous misfortune', produced good dividends.

"Pace Advertising have phoned," she informed me. "They want 40 reams of foolscap duplicating paper before lunch-time."

This was a very nice order, with quite a lot of money involved. Forty reams comes packed 10 in a carton, and with plenty of effort a man can just about hoist it up onto his shoulder and stagger in with it, so under normal circumstances it would take four journeys from the car to Pace's office on the fourth floor to complete the delivery. But this time the circumstances were not normal. I wouldn't be able to manage a carton with my arm in a sling so I would have to open them up and take in a box at a time. This would mean 40 trips up to the fourth floor.

'Thank goodness there's a lift,' I thought, as I began my first trip with the first box.

'Sorry lift out of order.'

The sign was there for all to see but I refused to believe it as I pressed the button frantically; but, yes, it was the awful truth. I had forty journeys up eight flights of stairs if I was to deliver my order.

No use looking at it, all I could do was get stuck in. My legs were wobbling an hour and a quarter later.

• • •

The business continued to prosper, and Judith and I were eagerly awaiting the birth of our first child. I could hardly contain myself with the excitement when she was finally admitted to hospital. The next day, 1st February, two days before my own birthday, Suzanne was born and the first time I saw her little face was the greatest moment in my life. I was thrilled three years later when my son Steven was born, but nothing could ever compare with my feelings as I looked at Suzanne for the first time.

I left the hospital with my mother, a happy and proud father, with the resolve to make the business go even better now that I had this extra little mouth to feed. I doubled my efforts and by June the sun was shining and business was good as I trekked around the town and bumped into Mr Muir again.

"Are you wantin' a shop?" he inquired in his familiar accent.

I had always wanted a shop. To play for City, to play for England, to have a son and to own a shop. Those were my life's ambitions.

I'd sort of accomplished the first, no chance now for the second, although my innersoles had. There was still time for the third and now I was being offered the fourth.

Mr Muir was offering me the little shop on Booth Street from where I'd bought my scrapbook years previously. I really fancied it, but as always it was a question of money.

"I want £450, but I want it straight away, no messing about, 450 smackers."

I just about had that amount of money, but a shop needed completely stocking out with all sorts of office requirements. If I was intending to go into anything I wanted to do it the correct way, no half measures. I would sooner turn down the opportunity rather than not do it properly. I said I would let him know. He kindly said that if I wanted, I could sit in the shop for a day to view the proceedings, so I took him up on his offer.

The Booth Street shop was very much secondary to his big one in St Peter's Square and I could tell Mr Muir just couldn't be bothered with it any more. The shelves were sparsely stocked, and it didn't look like good stock to me. The young lad who worked there lacked interest, and no thought seemed to have gone into the layout, but I felt inwardly excited as I began my day's observation.

I perched myself in a little corner of this tiny basement premises to await developments. The amount of traffic that entered the shop amazed me. There was a steady stream of customers coming down the stairs and making their way to the counter, only to be politely told whatever it was they required was out of stock before they made their way out again empty-handed. This went on all morning until I began to wonder if I would ever see a coin make its way over the counter and into the till, and by lunch-time it still hadn't happened.

After lunch, a local solicitor called in, strolled up to the counter and confidently asked,

"Do you have Bics?"

Now every stationer in the world stocks Bics. I could see a couple of boxes on the counter and so, at long last, I could witness a purchase being made, a transaction actually completed.

"Yes, we do," said the assistant with a smile.

"I'll have a red one please," requested the customer.

"Sorry, we only have blue or black," came the reply, and another unsatisfied customer made his exit.

I'd seen enough. If I can't do better than that then I'll pack up. I went straight to the bank, withdrew £450 and took it round to Mr Muir's to clinch the deal. It would be the best bit of business I would do in my life.

As the last week in June began I simply couldn't wait for Friday at five o'clock: Shaw's Stationers, as it was called, would close down and at one minute past I would begin my transformation.

I was fidgety all day long waiting for five o'clock to come. I was sitting in my car opposite the shop as I saw all the lights go out and as Mr Muir locked the door I strolled over and took the keys from him.

I was joined that evening by my parents, Auntie Sylvia, Uncle Arthur and my cousin Lynn, and between us we took that place apart. We began on Friday evening at 5.30, worked through until 2am and were back in action at 7.30 next morning. Over the weekend we were backwards and forwards from Lancaster Avenue, where I had been building up stock, to Booth Street, and at 8.30am on Monday 30th June 1969 my first shop opened for business.

The little shop was sparkling, a super new sign had been erected, and new shelving, courtesy of my dad's handiwork, was all packed out with brand-new stock. There was a lovely new floor, and the old display stands had been smartened up to look as good as new. In all, it was a complete transformation.

Booth Street was literally blocked with all the rubbish we had thrown out. I felt confident that we had done a great job and that the way I had planned the shop to make the most of what little space we had was correct. And I was right.

From the very first day the shop was a roaring success. The takings were more in the first day than in the entire month prior to me taking over. I was on a winner here. It was a feeling I had never known before, one of absolute confidence in the knowledge that I knew exactly what I was doing, knew where I was going, and barring any unforeseen catastrophes, I knew inwardly that I was on the threshold of something good. It was up to me from now on to make something happen from this small beginning.

I usually worked from six o'clock in the morning at the

shop until I closed at six o'clock in the evening. This wasn't exactly by choice, our daughter Suzanne simply did not sleep. Ever since the day she was born until the age of three she never slept for more than three hours any night.

From the age of three until five she was a little better, averaging about five hours a night, and when she became a teenager we couldn't get her up.

Invariably Judith and I were up at about five-thirty in the morning still trying to tire her out, so it was a waste of time me going back to bed — I simply went to work and completed all my paperwork with only the milkman to keep me company.

Things got so bad with Suzanne we took her to doctors and specialists, but nothing could be done, and we just had to wait for her to grow out of it.

In the meantime we had to send her to my mother's for a week every few months in order that we could get some sleep. Still, she made sure I was never late for work.

• • • •

Nineteen sixty-nine was also to be a good year on the soccer scene. I was, amazingly, back with a Football League club. Bradford Park Avenue were going through a particularly sticky time and had asked me to sign. They needed experienced players, but had no money to obtain any from other league clubs so had begun to look at non-league players.

The chairman of the club, an eccentric businessman called Herbert Metcalf, was based in Manchester. He knew of my pedigree and decided I was the man for them — I said he was eccentric. I went to see the manager, Don McAlman, and pledged with him to get Bradford Park Avenue out of the Fourth Division. This I succeeded in doing. I took them into the Northern Premier League.

That same evening I played against Notts County and while strolling to the ground I bought the local newspaper, only to find that I was to play right full-back. I'd played in many positions during my ten years as a pro but never at full-back, so it was going to be extra difficult, back among the full-time pros again and also in a strange position.

I stood outside the dressing-room for as long as I could, chatting to a former team-mate, Alan Smith, not really wanting to go in the dressing-room among all the full-timers, who must have been wondering who was going to be the occupant of that number two shirt left hanging on its peg.

Ten past seven, and I couldn't leave it any longer. Fifteen minutes before we were due on the field was very late anyway, so I took a deep breath and walked in. The sight that met me left me speechless. The scene was familiar from all the dozens of other dressing-rooms rooms I'd been in — clothes hanging everywhere, tie-ups strewn around, plasters, and the smell of oil and liniment. But the atmosphere was very different. It was very quiet. No noise, no chatter. The players were all sitting watching *This is Your Life* on television. They were stripped ready for the game but their eyes were glued to the set; Notts County were a mile from their thoughts.

I stood there transfixed, then I looked up at the set. I remember *Coronation Street* star Pat Phoenix was on but I'm not sure if she was a guest or the life subject. I then pulled myself together and quickly got changed. The referee's bell rang to signal us to make our way onto the field, but nobody moved a muscle until the refrain from the title music had died down. Only then did we all get to our feet and make our way down the stairs, through the bathroom and out onto the pitch. Unbelievable.

I enjoyed the game immensely and thought I played well. I felt really at home at full-back and only wished I'd moved there years earlier. I was always facing the play, I could see the whole picture and knew instinctively that I had found a new position. I stayed a full-back until I retired 10 years later. As usual I spent most of my time captaining the reserve team but was thoroughly enjoying my life back with a league club.

I was only at the club a short time but I played under four managers. I think they had a turnstile on the manager's door instead of hinges. Sadly Don McAlman soon lost his job and was followed by Ron Lewin, Frank Tomlinson and Tony Leighton. They used to write the manager's name on his office door in chalk at Park Avenue.

Ron, of the old-school-tie and plum-in-the-mouth brigade, looked down his nose at all us 'scrubbers' who couldn't play. He always left us with the impression that he was used to dealing with a better class of player. I'm sure he was.

I'd never heard of Frank Tomlinson. He was from Manchester. From Manchester and I'd never heard of him, it was inconceivable. He was a steward at a social club. I think somebody must have told Mr Metcalf he was a manager of a club and thinking they meant a football club he gave him the job, but in fairness he showed great judgement by selecting me for the first team away to high-flying Swansea.

Money was always a problem at Bradford. George Brigg,

the secretary, used to have an enormous alsatian dog in his office. I'm sure it was as a deterrent to stop players collecting their wages. It was always a problem getting paid; usually I didn't even bother attempting to collect mine.

One memorable week I played away at Middlesbrough on Tuesday and chased Irish international Johnny Crossan around Ayresome Park, arriving back home at three o'clock in the morning to be in the shop three hours later. I left for Swansea in a blizzard on Friday lunch-time, stayed Friday night at a hotel in Mumbles, got hammered by Swansea the next day, tried to mark Wales international Len Allchurch without much success, arrived home one o'clock on Sunday morning. Total pay for my endeavours and days off away from business: nothing, not one penny.

I didn't care, I loved every minute of it.

I had been with the club for three months when they told me that although they would like me to stay, they simply couldn't find the money for the signing-on fee they were obliged to pay me.

I told them that I didn't want it, but the Football League stated that I had to have it whether I wanted it or not, plus the same amount had to be paid to them. The total was £500 and the club simply did not have the cash, so until they paid up I was not allowed to play in the league team, only the reserves.

This was bad news for me. I wanted to stay, the club wanted me to stay—I should think so on that money—but I couldn't play because of this rule. There was nothing I could do.

It was decided that I would play for the reserve team in the mid-week league and be manager of the youth team in the intermediate league on Saturdays. I agreed, and so became a manager for the first time at the age of 25.

I was promised wages for my double job but rarely saw any. Even so, it was useful early experience handling young players (and their dads) and it stood me in good stead for future years. I was still playing at a good standard, so I was fairly happy and content. At the end of the season, Park Avenue were forced to apply for re-election and were not successful this time so were relegated to the Northern Premier League. A familiar stamping ground for me, so I was a useful person to retain on the staff for the next season.

I used to give lifts in my car back to Manchester to many youngsters and one evening after a game at Roker Park against Sunderland, I dropped about seven of these young hopefuls off in Piccadilly. I slowed down and they jumped out of my car and ran off to catch their respective buses home.

"Ta-ra," they called back as they sprinted away.

Only one boy, a slim, fresh-faced lad with a mass of blond curly hair, paused and said:

"Thank you very much for the lift," and I watched him dash off to catch up with the others.

On the strength of this alone I offered the lad a job at Fred Eyre Stationers when he left school a few weeks later. My judgement proved correct and Geoff Priestner eventually became a director of the company. I may not have been a shrewd judge of football talent, but I certainly knew a good stationer when I saw one.

TWENTY-SIX

Nearly as Many Businesses as Football Clubs

MY INSTINCT REGARDING THE POSSIBILITIES OF THE shop in Booth Street was fast proving to be correct, but all the while I was aware of two other stationers directly opposite me at number six, who, while they didn't have a shop front, seemed to do extraordinarily well.

Whenever a supplier delivered a big order to us, I would watch in amazement as he would deliver two or three times as much to them. I needed to investigate further. This was easier said than done; they were like invisible men. I never saw them. How they managed to do so well in business I couldn't imagine, but all of this stock constantly arriving must be being sold to somebody.

Eventually I discovered Mr Leech owned the two businesses, H.H. Ashworth Ltd and Holiday Taylor Ltd. He looked to be in his sixties. Mr Winstanley, who was probably in his forties, assisted him, and Mr Brannan, who looked after the accounts of these well-established businesses, was in his seventies. Not a very good half-back line but certainly formidable opposition on the business side.

The town wasn't big enough for both of us so I thought, 'If I can't wipe them out I'd better buy them out,' but my overtures fell on deaf ears. Soon afterwards, fate struck Mr Leech a cruel blow. He suffered a heart attack and couldn't carry on the business so he rang me and offered to sell.

I paid £15,000 to acquire the businesses of H.H. Ashworth and Holiday Taylor to go with the Shaw and Company shop and my own little Fred Eyre Stationers that I began with. I thought at that point I had reached the ultimate.

On the football side, Tony Leighton, a blunt Yorkshireman who was a brave centre-forward in his days with Huddersfield Town, Doncaster and Bradford City, had replaced Frank Tomlinson. Now nearing the end of his playing days, he swept into Park Avenue with the finesse of a charging rhino. I didn't like his style — screaming, shouting, and abusing his players. I used to sit back with a resigned look on my face as he slated each player in turn. I knew I would be on my travels again soon.

Tony, sadly for his family and friends, died from illness not long afterwards, which was a tragedy for such a fit man. He had boundless energy and was liked by many, but not really by me, and I was off to join Rossendale United.

Rossendale, with due respect to them, had been regarded for many years as a joke in their league. That was until Les Rigby took control and turned the club inside out. Les, a big, burly ex-centre-half for Lytham, knew non-league football inside out. He knew every player, no matter how obscure, his strengths, his weaknesses, even what he had for breakfast. Les impressed me immensely. He was a physical training instructor at Wigan Technical College who became a close friend, but this day he was my prospective manager as he prepared to smooth-talk me into signing for his team, which had romped away with the Cheshire League the previous season.

"Can't see you getting into a great side like this but I'd like you in my squad. Also, the money is fairly low."

"How low?" I enquired.

"Sod all," he said. "Until I release somebody, then you can have his wages."

"Sod all," I mused. "That is pretty low, Les."

But I signed nevertheless because of him and I'm glad I did.

I loved it at Rossendale. The ground had seen better days, the changing accommodation left a lot to be desired, but the players were great. We were a bunch of misfits, me included, but Les, with great perception, saw each individual's strengths. We had one thing in common: we all had something missing but we could all play. We all had skill, and while other clubs may not have been able to harness it, Les knew exactly what he wanted and utilised our assets to make a great team. I was proud to be part of it.

We did well in the league, finishing runners up. Maybe the reason we did not win it is because we also surpassed ourselves in a few cup competitions, always playing teams higher than us, but always winning whether we were drawn at home or away. This took its toll and we dropped a couple of silly points near the end to finish runners up.

We also triumphed to become that season's giant killers in the FA Cup, reaching the fourth round before being beaten by Bolton Wanderers 1–4. I had played in the earlier rounds and helped us reach this momentous occasion but, as in the past, I got a sickener when we played a 'nothing' game the week before. I went in for another reckless tackle. I knew instinctively that I was in trouble as soon as I made the tackle, when I stood on one leg in the centre circle and saw my other leg wafting about from side to side in the night breeze. Not backwards and forwards like everybody else's does, but swinging loosely from side to side as if hanging on a thread. I knew it was a long job so I didn't even wait for the game to stop. I simply hopped to the touch-line and up the tunnel into the dressing-room. I was out of the game for 12 weeks and out of Saturday's big game with Bolton Wanderers.

I was forced to watch the game from the touch-line with broken-leg victim David Crompton, our flying left-winger who became the manager of England Schoolboys. We ripped into our famous opponents from the kick-off. The game had been switched to Gigg Lane, Bury's ground, to accommodate the 17,000 crowd and while driving to the ground, my pal John Clay, an inside-forward who was with me at City, was obviously thinking I was feeling a bit left out of things. He turned to me on the coach and said:

"If I score I will come racing over to the dug-out so you can join in the celebrations."

"Okay," I smiled at his optimism, but sure enough, with only 17 minutes gone he broke through, past centre-half Paul Jones, drew keeper Charlie Wright off his line and calmly slotted it past him for the opening goal. The crowd roared as he, true to his word, came charging across to me on the bench. It was a jubilant moment and even though we eventually crumbled to a Roy Greaves hat-trick, the boys did themselves proud and gave us all a day to remember.

I was back for all the other cup finals and won a hatful

of trophies with Rossendale. One of the finals had to be postponed an hour before the kick-off because the weather suddenly changed, and unfortunate though it was, the referee was perfectly correct to postpone the game. On hearing this, one of the Rossendale committee calmly walked into the referee's room and remonstrated with him.

"You can't call this game off, referee, it's totally out of the question. The game simply has to be played because we've ordered extra pies."

We had some great times at Rossy.

While I was there I realised what a great boost to my career the substitute rule had been. I think it extended my career by about 10 years. When we used to arrive at away grounds the players went to inspect the pitch to see which studs they should wear. I inspected the bench. Was it wooden? Or was there a chair, with maybe a cushion provided if it was a really luxurious ground? After games, the other lads would be having treatment for blistered feet, I was having the same treatment for my backside.

One of my managers began to question my ability to last the full 90 minutes and thought that it would be a good tactic to substitute me after 70 minutes, and bring on a fresh young pair of legs for the final 20 minutes of the game. I personally did not think this was a very good idea. Undeterred, he proceeded to hook me off before the end for six consecutive games, until I decided to do something about it. Just before we left the dressing-room to start the second half, I nicked the 'number 3' card from his set of numbers and hid it in the toilet. I thoroughly enjoyed myself for the second period of the game until I saw our trainer standing on the touch-line

20 minutes from the end holding the white inside of an Elastoplast box aloft, with '3' scribbled on it in biro.

When they want you off that badly you just have to go as gracefully as possible.

•

Rossendale United provided my first soccer trip abroad. Les Rigby organised a fantastic trip to New York in 1972. I'd never been abroad before but it was to be the first of many more trips, which brought me 42 games in 19 countries around the world. They have all been marvellous but that first one will always be special.

We played six games in and around the New York area: Orange Grove, New Jersey; Greenwich Village; Hartford, Connecticut; Falls River; Philadelphia; and a game against New York Cosmos at the Hofstra Stadium. This gave me a unique opportunity to witness the progress of American soccer five years later because I am one of the few players to play against them at their outset at the Hofstra in 1972 and then again in 1977 when they had advanced at an alarming rate, after the signing of Pelé, to the mighty Giants Stadium in New Jersey.

It was a tremendous experience for me to lead my team out into this huge bowl-shaped arena with its gigantic scoreboard welcoming us to 'The Cosmos'. The ground shone like a new pin and the dressing-rooms resembled the most luxurious Swiss clinic. Moving staircases on the exterior of the ground took the spectators to their seats. The artificial astroturf was as level as a Subbuteo board, and the all-seater stadium, which could hold 77,000, is set in its own grounds surrounded by a giant car park to hold thousands and thousands of cars. To view the stadium in the distance as you drive towards it, knowing that within the hour you will be performing there, is a breathtaking sight.

But that was five years later. My first game against the Cosmos was in June 1972 on the University campus. It was a nice little ground with good facilities but nothing to compare with where they would move to in the future.

The game was memorable for me because in a 3–1 win I scored all the goals. Not bad for a left-back, but they were all penalties. It was strange how many penalties we were given in these matches abroad; we seemed to be awarded one almost every other game. I accepted the responsibility and happily slotted every one in.

All the games on this tour were memorable. We kicked off the first one within an hour of reaching J.F. Kennedy Airport. We had flown halfway round the world, struggled through customs with our luggage only to be told we were kicking off within the hour. So, luggage and all, we arrived at the ground for the first game at Jones Beach, New York. We didn't even have time for a wash before we were lining up to kick off in a heatwave. It was like a furnace and it took me quite a time to catch my breath, but it was a tremendous game, which, in spite of our taking an early lead, we eventually lost 3–4. Jet lag was our excuse. The pitch was next to the famous beach with its white sands and rolling waves. At the end of the game we declined the dressing-room facilities and chose instead to bathe in the sea, still wearing our kit.

My partner at full-back on this trip was David Brooks, a

well-known local amateur player who is a very successful solicitor in his private life. He is five feet five inches but would be six feet two if his legs were straight. He has red hair, like me, only not as much, and we looked a fiery combination. I think we complemented each other very well. He provided the thrust—he was very quick, marked his winger like a leech, won nearly all his tackles and then passed the ball into the crowd. I provided the guile, a little on the slow side, but I read the game well and was a good passer of the ball. If we each also possessed the other's assets we would be great players.

Nevertheless, we were a good partnership and we went on to play hundreds of games together all over the world. When I was appointed coach at Wigan Athletic a few years later, the Boss, Ian McNiell, said I could have an assistant, provided he was honest, had a good character, a sound knowledge of the game and had been a top player himself. Three out of four isn't bad, so Brooky was offered the job.

. . .

Back home, my private life continued to prosper and business was still improving. I had endured many major national crises and still come up smiling but there were one or two more still to come.

There had been three big increases in purchase tax. Each one meant big problems for me. This was eventually replaced by VAT, which caused immense worry. The pound was devalued and we had the three-day week. People had to work three days, on the instructions of the Government. This was a blow to some of my mates because prior to this they only worked two days.

There were 'black-outs' when the miners went on strike. We never knew when we were going to be plunged into darkness, which is obviously a problem for a shopkeeper, plus all the heating and electricity went off without warning. This meant if the electric till happened to be closed when we were cut off we couldn't open it again to give customers their change. They still came in to buy, though, even in the dark.

Then there was decimalisation, the biggest problem of all. I had done everything possible to ensure a smooth changeover but the success of it depended on me being there. The day before the big day, I was struck down with glandular fever and was really ill for a fortnight. It had to be bad for me to miss the day that was going to put Britain on its knees.

But I survived these history-making moments. We had moved house a couple of years previously, from Radcliffe to Whitefield, a very classy area about three miles away, and were now looking for another, larger house because five weeks before my American trip my son, Steven Frederick Eyre, was born.

This was another momentous occasion in my life. I had got used to having a daughter and was convinced that we would have another girl, so I was both surprised and over-joyed when I was told it was a boy. My first sight of him was a big disappointment. I was quite taken aback. Suzanne had looked so perfect and lovely that I thought all babies looked that way, so I was shocked to see Steven, wrinkled and yellow, lying in his cot. It quite upset me. Thankfully he soon pulled himself round and developed into a fine young boy, a very talented young footballer, with a lovely natural left foot, who played for his school at a record early age. Now that sounds familiar.

We eventually moved to a lovely house in Worsley, a very prestigious area of Manchester, a little in the country but close enough for me to travel into the city. I love it in Worsley and don't think I will ever leave the area.

. . .

The main competition to Fred Eyre Stationers was a large shop round the corner on Princess Street, a main thoroughfare running alongside the Town Hall. It was well established and situated in this prime position. The owner, Mr Crichton, was not a young man, so I made an appointment to see him with a view to purchasing his business. The deal went smoothly and I obtained this prestigious establishment for £25,000.

I now owned five stationery businesses all within a radius of about 50 yards. It seemed a rather bizarre situation even to me, but each one was successful so I simply carried on. Buying stock for five companies enabled me to obtain the best possible terms from my suppliers and any extra profits I made in this way I attempted to share with my customers by keeping my prices as reasonable as possible.

Company number six came my way with the purchase of a small stationery business in Poynton, near Stockport, which I immediately absorbed into the other five.

I felt that this was enough companies because I didn't want to lose the personal touch and service that had always been my trademark, so I entered a period of consolidation, happy and contented with my lot.

I was not happy and contented with my football, however. I was now 30, the age when everybody says you are finished as a player, and I believed them. It is an attitude of mind and I must admit that my mind was invariably focused on my business, which is not surprising because it was producing lucrative rewards, and not on my football.

I occasionally missed training sessions, which was not like me at all. I wasn't the fittest player but I prided myself on being the most reliable. Due to the extra work involved in running all six companies this was no longer the case and it occurred to me that it would be a good idea to finish playing and if possible remain in the game in some different capacity, as a hobby.

TWENTY-SEVEN

Just Managing

TWO OF MY CLOSEST FRIENDS, BOBBY SMITH FROM WAY back in my Ducie Avenue days, and George Smith, a loveable Irish goalkeeper who took me under his wing at Buxton, each secured a job in football at this time.

Bob became coach and subsequently manager of Bury Football Club, and, at 28, was the youngest manager in the Football League at that time. George became manager of Cheshire League side Stalybridge Celtic. Both of them recognised talent when they saw it, as each offered me a job on their staff.

In view of my business commitments, and the fact that I wanted to take things easy—I accepted both jobs. I trained the Stalybridge lads on Tuesday and Thursday evenings and took charge of Bury's Central League team on Saturdays. If it had been good enough for Bally's dad, then it was good enough for me.

The Bury set-up was great and there were many promising lads in the team who went on to do very well in the game. I enjoyed being back among the full-time pros, but the grumpy chairman never really made me feel welcome. I don't think he had ever come across anybody quite like me in football before, so he was a little bit suspicious, a little bit wary of me.

I had acquired for myself a lovely Rolls Royce by this time, with a personalised SFE1 number plate, for when I eventually received my knighthood. I don't think that he could really comprehend that there was no hidden agenda and I was just there, for free, to help my old pal Bob in his first job in football management.

At Stalybridge, I respected the manager, George Smith, just as I loved Bob at Bury. He was a chatterbox, who talked football morning, noon and night, and a very hard-working boss. I was sponge-man at Stalybridge, rubbing the legs and generally looking after the needs of the players, and I was also involved with the training and coaching. I thoroughly enjoyed it but eventually George's talents were recognised by the people of Iceland and he was off to further his career in football.

I was ready to leave as well, because I really worked for George, not Stalybridge Celtic, and was preparing to do so when I was offered the job of manager. I was very flattered but I declined immediately. To be a manager of a football club was the last thing I wanted.

Despite this, we all have our weak spots and my vanity was pricked when the players held a meeting to present a deputation to the board of directors requesting me as their manager. This was simply too much for my ego and I finally accepted the post. Unfortunately I regretted it from almost the very first minute.

I have always been very professional in everything I have ever tried to do, and never needed to be carried around and wet-nursed in the way that George had done with some of the team. It was George's way to do absolutely everything for his players. He even instructed them on what to eat, even though half of them sank about six pints of lager a night in their spare time. I wasn't prepared to do this. I pinned a team sheet up onto the notice board with the departure time typed on and did not expect to be aroused from my slumbers by a call from a telephone box at two o'clock in the morning to be asked,

"What time does the coach leave tomorrow?"

Some of the players came to me about every stupid little thing. They were much, much worse than the famous pros with whom I had dealt in the past. I really disliked the job but did not have the heart to resign after such a short time.

The results on the field were reasonable and I sold 20-year-old Eammon O'Keefe to Plymouth Argyle for a reported club-record fee, which helped to pay for the floodlights. So in my 11 weeks in charge my record was respectable and we made a huge profit.

Judith, in the meantime, had been having serious problems with her throat. We had tried every cure except a rope or a razor, so she was admitted to hospital for an operation. Six businesses, two young children and a football team to look after with my wife in hospital. It was just the excuse I needed, so I immediately handed in my resignation. It was accepted, it said in the press, 'with regret'. I could have coped but I didn't want to; I was glad to be away. George Smith was the main difference. I loved it when George was there and hated it when he wasn't.

Not long after, I met a man called Chris Davies, who obviously thought I was too young not to be playing and felt that I still had something to offer. He invited me to join his team, a select band of amateurs who toured abroad every close season under the banner 'Manchester AFC' and played in tournaments all around the world each summer. He said they could do with somebody with my experience to play in the team. We played games in Spain and Morocco. The experience whetted my appetite again and I thoroughly enjoyed it all. We were treated like kings, escorted round the Palace in Morocco and generally had a fine time.

Chris Davies has done more than anybody I know to promote local amateur soccer and is one of the game's finest administrators. His trips were always superbly organised and the one trip to Spain and Morocco was followed by tours to Jamaica, Haiti, Cuba, the Bahamas, the United States (many times), Canada, Barbados, Trinidad, Tobago, France, Belgium, Kenya, Tanzania and most of the European countries. I love to travel and I always did my best to ensure that Chris selected me for the next trip, until the day came when I had to admit that I was simply too old. That was a sad day for me and hopefully for Chris too.

Half-time

(The World is my Lobster)

TWENTY-EIGHT

Jamaica, Cuba, Haiti, Nassau, Los Angeles, Las Vegas, Australia

JAMAICA WAS A PLACE I FOUND RATHER UNNERVING. It is a lovely island but I could sense an undercurrent of violence just below the surface.

The team was allocated three luxurious houses next door to one another on Patterson Avenue in Montego Bay; each had its own swimming pool, with a maid, cook and gardener to each villa.

Our first game was actually in Montego Bay, which we won, but only after we had helped the officials to remove a stubborn cow that simply refused to move from the pitch.

We moved on to Kingston, the capital of Jamaica, where I sensed some hostility towards us. The night before the game I was sitting in a café having a bedtime cup of coffee to quench an everlasting thirst before retiring for the night. I was sitting with Dave Brooks chatting about the forthcoming game when a local Jamaican youth sidled up to me, gave a quick glance over each shoulder and whispered to me from out of the corner of his mouth:

"Say, man, do you want coke?"

I looked up, startled to be approached in this strange place.

"No thanks, I just ordered this coffee," I replied naively.

He retreated scratching his head, obviously thinking how stupid these Englishmen were.

My fears regarding the violence were confirmed as we stood in the tunnel waiting to take the field to play the national team at the National Stadium, a fantastic complex, where the Commonwealth Games had been held and where Smokin' Joe Frazier was knocked out by George Foreman when he lost the Heavyweight Championship of the World.

We could have done with him on our side that night because before we even reached the pitch we were subjected to a revolting deluge as the crowd proceeded to spit all over us as we took the field.

We had two players sent off and our goalkeeper, Roy Davies, carried off as we literally battled our way to an honourable 0–0 draw. Even with the depleted team, I would have died rather than let them score. I was disappointed that we hadn't won but was delighted that under the circumstances they hadn't won either.

It was midnight as we left the stadium and we faced a six-hour coach journey through the jungle back to Montego Bay. The journey out had been horrendous, up mountains, over bumpy roads, round narrow bends and over streams, and after the efforts of the game I simply couldn't bear to even think about doing it again, so I decided, along with Brooky, to invest in an overnight stay at an hotel and a flight back to Montego Bay in the morning.

I paid for this little perk myself, of course, but I thought I deserved a bit of luxury after working hard all my life, and even though I felt I really should have stayed with the team, I enjoyed a good night's sleep instead.

The following morning as I tucked into a hearty breakfast I was informed in a quite matter-of-fact manner that a man had been murdered outside my bedroom window while I had slept like a baby.

Perhaps I should have gone with the team after all.

Cuba

After the treatment we incurred in Kingston, some of the players were a little reluctant to venture into the unknown of Communist Cuba and a meeting was held in my bedroom. I was alarmed to see, after a show of hands, that only half were in favour of going.

I thought we could be in serious trouble if we went back on our word and I persuaded the doubters to make the trip. It's a good job we decided to go, because there was a big reception party waiting to meet us at the airport in Havana, although even this couldn't cut us through all the red tape.

There were dreary black-and-white pictures of Fidel Castro and Che Guevara in shabby frames all over the airport, and endless military men in faded khaki uniforms wandered about sporting guns and grim faces. We were finally escorted through to our coach. It was even more ramshackle than the aircraft we had just left, which I'm sure had an outside toilet.

The thing that struck me most as we drove through deserted, drab streets was the lack of any advertising. The boards were all there but they didn't say 'Beanz Meanz Heinz' or 'My Goodness My Guinness', but simply reminded the inhabitants of Havana what a great life it was in Cuba and how much Mr Castro was doing for his people.

We reached the Hotel National on the tip of the coast. We

could see Miami in the distance and thought how different things were only a few miles across the sea. The Hotel National was a huge place in poor repair and in need of a lot of restoration work. Only the first two floors were used and it was with a little trepidation that we made our way to our rooms.

I was in Cuba for three days and in all the time there I never ate one single scrap of food, it was absolutely appalling. Most of my time was spent walking the streets and sitting by the hotel pool, but not for long because the heat was unbearable.

Each time I left the hotel I was besieged by young boys asking me for chewing gum, an unavailable commodity there, and by adults wanting my T-shirts or any other garment from the western world.

My main hobby when I am abroad is scouring the local shops. I love going out on my own, looking for unusual objets d'art for our home, and different styles and items of clothing for Judith, the children and myself, as well as gifts for my mother and father. I had no chance of doing this in Havana; there was no private enterprise whatsoever and we had to ask for the whole team to go en masse to a state-owned shop to buy our gifts.

Even this was not as simple as it sounds. Everything in Cuba was about five years behind in style to the Europeans and Americans. So obviously Brooky's suit was the height of fashion in Havana.

The game itself was an eye-opener. The Stadium Latin Americana was magnificent, a huge arena which seated about 50,000 people, and we were amazed to find it nearly full as we left the dressing-rooms. It was only afterwards that we discovered that all sport is free in Cuba, so it was a free night out for the locals and they had not paid out any hard-earned pesos to see us in action.

Our opponents, the Cuban national team, were a fine side. They were very fit and fast, and they gave us quite a chasing. We were the first British team ever to have played in Cuba so we weren't prepared when they ripped into us from the kick-off. Television cameras recorded our every move. They were even in our dressing-room at half-time and the end of the game; it was a good job they couldn't speak English when we gave vent to our feelings at the end. During the game Cuba were awarded a penalty, and it was at this point that I was paid the greatest compliment I have ever had regarding my knowledge of the game. As soon as the spot-kick had been awarded, our silver-haired goalkeeper, the extrovert Roy Davies, walked slowly from his goal-line to where I stood on the edge of the penalty area and enquired:

"Which side does he put them?"

The only team ever to have played in Cuba and he expected me to know which side the number six put his penalties. I tried to keep my reputation intact by taking a wild guess at 'your left', and then stood helpless as Roy took my advice and dived hopelessly the wrong way. The look he gave me as he fished the ball out of the net was enough to kill.

Roy, always with good intentions, no matter what obscure corner of the world we were playing in, always came to me in the dressing-room before the game and with a slow shake of the head never failed to inform me that he had heard that the winger I was about to mark could 'catch pigeons'.

Everywhere we went, my winger apparently was a flier. It was about time I made him suffer for a change.

I was delighted to leave Cuba the next day, but not before we had to endure a conducted tour of building sites, schools being built, flats being constructed, all propaganda sights that we didn't want to see. Whenever I, as the official spokesman, asked to be taken to see something of interest, like where Fidel lived or anything of world-wide importance, it fell on deaf ears. The nearest I got was a seat in the tank that Castro used on his triumphant journey through the town after he had overthrown the old regime. To do this I had to be accompanied by an armed guard who looked as though he was dying to receive an order from his superior to blow my head off.

Haiti

Haiti was a different proposition altogether. It has a long history of uprisings and revolutions. The memory of Papa Doc and his son Baby Doc dominated the island and there was an air of fear about the place, which I sensed as soon as we landed at the airport at Port-au-Prince.

My first sight as I came through customs was a huge poster of myself and my team-mates, advertising the forthcoming game. I realised it was to be an important fixture.

We had a police escort from the airport to our hotel. Motorcycles with their sirens blaring flanked our three huge limousines as we roared through the narrow streets and it was hard luck for anybody who couldn't get out of the way quick enough. One particularly vivid memory I have is of a woman, one of many, who was washing her hair in the gutter as the muddy, filthy water flowed along the side of the street. She was oblivious to the noise and commotion of our arrival and was on her hands and knees rinsing her hair as the car in which I was a passenger raced towards her. I was helpless in the front passenger seat as the wheels of the car actually ran over her hair, missing crushing her head by a couple of inches. I had the distinct impression that human life counted for very little in Haiti.

The next morning we went to the Stade Silvio Cator stadium for a training session and 3,000 people turned up simply to watch us train; a few discreet enquiries revealed that there is so little to do in Haiti that even our training session was regarded as a big event.

We played the national champions, Violette FC, who were very skilful players in their own right, but they had reinforced their team for the occasion with three Argentinean internationals, so they provided formidable opposition.

The game was televised live in Haiti and also broadcast across the island. Brooky was the only French-speaking player in the squad and was in great demand for after-match interviews, speaking on behalf of all the players.

I don't know what he told them but he certainly got the best mentions in the newspapers the next day.

Nassau

Nassau in the Bahamas really was a beautiful place to play football; our games on this island kicked off at eight o'clock in the evening when it was just cool enough to enjoy the game.

I was interviewed one glorious sunny day for Bahama Radio outside our hotel on Paradise Island and as I answered the interviewer's many questions I could see over his shoulder a huge sign saying 'Welcome to Paradise'. I remember thinking how right that was.

The games were highly competitive and thoroughly enjoyable; we played their league champions and a Representative XI of the whole league. I was happy with my form, even though I wasn't getting any younger, and nicked in with a couple of my usual penalties.

The opposition was well coached and organised due to a number of ex-professionals from Britain who were out there passing on their knowledge to the locals.

From there we flew across to Miami to take part in a tournament with teams from Peru, Honduras and Haiti. Again, the main problem was the heat. Teams played each other over a long weekend, so we played a match every day in midday heat reaching 92 degrees. We acquitted ourselves very well under the circumstances and came an honourable runner-up to Haiti, who received the trophy.

I played games in many parts of America and loved every one of my trips. Each visit to the 'land of opportunity' convinces me that we are slipping further and further behind in this country. I have found the service and value for money to be much superior to ours.

Mind you, I did encounter one or two problems while in America.

Los Angeles

On one visit to Los Angeles we arrived at the airport to find the suitcase of my room-mate had gone astray. Everyone else had been cleared at customs and was on their way to the hotel, but, being the good pal I am, I hung about the airport lounge while he desperately searched for his missing case. I was standing all by myself, taking in the scene of this crowded famous airport, wondering if any well-known actor or actress would come drifting through, when there was a loud bang. I didn't really pay much attention until it was followed by another bang. This second bang was accompanied by frantic, panic-stricken people rushing, running, jumping and diving in all directions of the airport, until I was the only bemused person left standing there. If any of my former managers had seen me at that moment it would have confirmed all their opinions that I was slow. I just couldn't take it all in as I stood transfixed, simply unable to move. Old ladies with walking sticks whizzed past me but I was rooted to the spot.

Coming from dear old Blighty, these things just did not happen; it couldn't possibly have been a gunshot. I looked around quickly to ascertain what all the fuss was about. I found out quickly enough as I saw a gargantuous black woman waving a gun about, firing in all directions, a mad crazed look in her unseeing eyes. I was only 15 feet away from her and there were only the two of us in the room, but she was so crazy she didn't see me as she charged about like a huge enraged bull.

I was now in possession of all my faculties, indeed they were working overtime, as my Blackley instincts for survival searched desperately for an escape route. I dived head first down behind my upright suitcase, rolled over onto my back and reviewed the position. It didn't look much better from down there. The situation was grim and all I could see and hear were her huge feet as they flapped about on the tiled floor like a pair of frogman's flippers. As I lay there wondering how long it would be before she spotted me, I realised there was another person present in the room. I was horrified to see a little baby, sitting quietly upright in its buggy idly playing with its beads. A quick check revealed the mad woman was at the far end of the room, so I was up onto my knees—a quick, crouched dash ought to be enough to grab the baby and get back before I was spotted. It was only when I was in mid-dash in the middle of no man's land that I realised that the child was strapped in. I didn't have time to mess about so I upturned the trolley, baby and all, and dragged the lot back to the sanctuary of my hiding place behind the suitcase, hoping this sudden upset wouldn't set it off crying.

A quick release of the harness left my new companion and I lying behind the case, which is where we remained for what seemed a lifetime as the woman continued to shoot at will. My new friend was muttering in my ear:

"I don't like the bang bang."

"I'm not too keen on it myself," I replied as I patted its back in an attempt to keep it quiet.

Seconds later the automatic airport doors flew open and two police officers rushed in, guns in hand, crouched positions, and began to circle the room. One of them spotted us on the floor and looked at me with a mixture of anger and astonishment.

"What the hell are you doing here?" he screamed at me.

I didn't really answer. I just looked blankly at him and said: "I'm just stuck here."

Not really one of the scintillating replies for which I am famous, but the best I could do under the circumstances.

"Well get the hell out of it," he commanded.

He scared me a bit by his fierceness but not as much as she did with her gun, so I told him:

"I don't fancy making a run for it, I'll take my chance lying down here."

When an American policeman tells you to do something he expects you to do it, especially when he's brandishing a gun, and, obviously not intending to argue with me, he grabbed my leg and, with the baby balanced on my chest, dragged me across the floor towards the door. I moved quite sweetly across the shiny tiled floor, even though my best jacket took a bit of a pounding, but it was a little more difficult as I was bounced across the rubber doormat, along the sidewalk about 20 yards and left prostrate among the thronging Californian pedestrians, still clutching the baby to my chest.

"Now will you get to hell?" he shouted over his shoulder as he raced back to help his mate overthrow the lunatic.

He didn't have far to go. She had spotted us leaving the scene and was charging after us.

I felt like the fugitive as I scrambled to my feet with the

baby, who seemed by now to weigh a ton, and I dashed across the freeway, dodging between huge limousines bearing down on us.

As I scrambled away with the baby I was convinced that some do-gooder pedestrian who didn't know what was really going on would think I had snatched a baby and was running away with it, accost me and hand me back to my friendly policeman.

As I was crouched down behind the wheel of a parked Greyhound bus, wondering in which direction to dash next, I saw the two cops wrestle the mad woman to the ground. In the ensuing struggle, which took quite a while because she was so strong, her big blonde wig rolled from out of the scrimmage and settled in the gutter. I was convinced that her head had been chopped off; it simply never occurred to me she was wearing a wig as I watched the tussle, gasping for my breath.

As she was finally overpowered and handcuffed, the stark horror of her madness revealed itself. One passenger re-appeared with a bullet in his head, one airport official had two bullets in his arm and one man had been shot in the back. A portable hospital arrived with drips and hospital beds as an emergency unit was set up.

I stood and watched the scene unfold from a short distance away, still unable to believe it had all actually happened. I didn't realise I still had the baby in my arms until there was a tap on my shoulder and a man said quietly,

"That's my son you've got there."

I didn't say a word, just numbly handed the boy over, never to see him again. A couple of weeks later I received a letter from Stephen's parents in Hampshire—I don't know how they found my address—thanking me for my efforts.

This slightly embarrassed me because I knew inwardly that I'd done it all without thinking and if I had had time to think I probably wouldn't have done it at all. But I wrote back saying I was glad Stephen was okay and it was only the normal sort of thing that any superhero would have done.

Meanwhile Georgina Washington, aged 43, was charged with attempted multiple murders. I just hoped they didn't want me to go back for the trial. I'd had quite enough of those already during my career so far, thank you very much. I had come here to play football, not to get involved in an episode of *Starsky and Hutch*.

After our game in Los Angeles, I had arranged to meet my pal, singing star Malcolm Roberts, who had invited me to stay with him for a few days.

Malcolm had enjoyed considerable success in England with his good looks and powerful singing voice and after hitting the charts with a couple of singles, had decided to try his luck in America, following the success of Tom Jones and Englebert Humperdinck.

He met me at the Beverly Hilton Hotel, where else? And before jet lag and post-match rigor mortis could set in, he had whisked me off to a party at the house of a sultry American female singer. It was my first trip to the capital of Cardboard California so I was not yet used to being surrounded by gleaming teeth, and people hoping that I 'have a nice day' when really they couldn't give a toss. Nor was I used to being served breakfast or coffee by an aspiring actor who had just sent his ten-by-eight glossies off to the William Morris agency.

Still, I had no worries. I was with my old mate Malc. He would look after me. He certainly seemed to have adjusted to his new lifestyle very easily. The sun had bleached his flowing mane and his snow-white trousers looked as though they had been sprayed on. His flowered shirt, with the correct number of buttons left undone, revealed a discreet little medallion the size of a digestive biscuit, and his shirt collar, of course, was in the upright position. He had an even tan and molars that, while not being the genuine Hollywood reconstruction job, were certainly in better shape than when he used to go to that National Health dentist near Crumpsall Hospital.

Provided he didn't topple off his white, patent-leather, Cuban-heeled boots, he would be okay, and I felt very comfortable alongside him, in the short-sleeved shirt my mother had got for me from Conran Street market and my grey slacks with matching shoes from Freeman Hardy and Willis.

Two carboys came to park our car.

"I've forgotten how to put a car into reverse since I came here," Malc confessed as we rang the bell.

"Darling," the door was opened by a set of teeth.

"This is my mate Fred from England," Malcolm announced.

"Darling," the teeth said to me, while gazing over my shoulder to see if anybody really worth knowing was following behind. We went in, and that was the last I saw of Malcolm until it was time to go home.

I found a little corner for myself and proceeded to watch

the world go by. The jet lag still eluded me. Various concoctions were put into my hand and beautiful people drifted by. Many sets of pearlies were flashed in my direction, as various visions passed before my eyes, but nobody stopped to utter a word to me. Nobody even hoped I'd 'have a nice day'. Actually I felt quite content; I was mildly amused by the antics of those around me, and I was quietly enjoying my little self, seeing how the other half lived.

I was feeling quite relieved that I would only be part of it for five or six hours before returning to the real world when this lovely young lady obviously decided that I had been sitting on my own for long enough. Being a gentleman, and a well-brought-up Blackley boy into the bargain, I got to my feet as she approached and this show of typically olde English good manners cost me a searing pain in my right knee as two cartilages clicked like castanets in the Edmundo Ros Orchestra. She was obviously a good-hearted young woman and felt sorry for this poor old guy sitting alone in the corner, and I gave her full marks for making the effort.

I thought that she was possibly training for a job with the Samaritans, so I went along with it as she struggled to find a bit of common ground, so that after a suitable length of time she would be able to go off and mingle with the rest of the crowd, comforted by the knowledge that she had done her good deed for the day.

"I really like your trousers," she said in a cut-glass English accent.

I had to give the girl credit; she was doing her best. There we were, surrounded by athletic young actors and slim male models parading in gear freshly bought and tailored on Rodeo

Drive that very morning, and she was admiring a pair of creased gabardine slacks with a copy of *Charles Buchan's Football Monthly* jutting out of the back pocket.

"They're from an exclusive little boutique," I joked.

"In Chelsea?"

She had made her big mistake; she had mentioned the name of a football team. Any team would have suited me, but I was quite happy with Chelsea, and we spent the next half-hour discussing Stamford Bridge, Peter Osgood, Charlie Cooke, Peter Bonetti, and I even threw in Roy Bentley and Eric Parsons from the 1950s for good measure.

What a game girl.

She tried her best to look interested as I rattled on. She may not have done before, but she sure knew the difference between 4–2–4 and 4–3–3 by the time I'd finished. She kept nodding in most of the wrong places, constantly stroking her hair with one hand, while stifling a yawn with the other.

Actually her hair was her most striking feature, flowing all the way down her back. She had a beautiful oval face, lovely skin, big eyes, a voice like velvet and perfect teeth that looked natural. In fact she looked like a film star. But film stars are too wrapped up in themselves to feel sorry for some geezer from England whose mate has left him on his own in a strange house in a strange country 3,000 miles from home. Film stars are not that considerate, they only think of themselves, don't they?

I think it was when I was discussing the far-post crosses of Frank Blunstone and the goal-scoring instincts of Bobby Tambling that she decided that she had done her bit for England and moved effortlessly away in search of food.

At this point Malcolm decided to renew his acquaintance with me.

"You and Jane seem to be getting along very well, was she telling you how much she misses England?"

"Is that her name?" I replied. "I was just educating her about the history of Chelsea Football Club."

Malcolm, obviously despairing of me, decided it was time to go.

I will say this though. If Jane Seymour ever becomes fed up of playing sexy Bond girls on the silver screen, or Wallis Simpson, Marie Antoinette or Maria Callas in 'mini-blockbusters' on our TV screens, she could always become a social worker, hospital visitor or any similar job that requires kindness and patience. Or for that matter, she could even become the official statistician for Chelsea Football Club — she certainly knows enough about it now.

Las Vegas

One of the highlights of this tour was a trip to the gambling capital of the world. We had two free days to do what we wanted, and Pete Tattersall and I decided to fly to Las Vegas to see the sights.

Peter is a successful record producer in his own right, so is quite used to mixing with top show-business stars, but even he was not prepared for the events of the next few hours.

We boarded the plane at Los Angeles airport at 10 o'clock in the evening for the 55-minute flight to this oasis of neon lights and slot machines in the middle of the Nevada Desert. I was browsing through the in-flight magazine when I noticed that Frank Sinatra was appearing at the famous Caesar's Palace. I'm not a fan of Frank Sinatra's but if you are going to Las Vegas then Caesar's Palace with Frank Sinatra is the only place to go. Like those people who never go to football matches, but Liverpool versus Manchester United at Wembley is a must on their social calendar.

I told Peter that this was where we must go that evening, a comment that brought much mirth from the occupant of the other seat in our row. Apparently tickets had been sold out many months previously and if you didn't have a ticket then you had no chance. Even if you had a ticket it sounded as though you would be lucky to get in.

Undeterred, we decided to go anyway and asked the cab driver to take us there without delay, because Ol' Blue Eyes was due on stage in 20 minutes.

"Hope you guys have got tickets," the cab driver said to us as we told him our intended destination.

"We didn't even know he was appearing until 15 minutes ago," we replied.

"You'd be better off staying in the cab with me," he guffawed as he dropped us off outside the imposing entrance of Caesar's.

As we entered this gambler's paradise the scene took my breath away. There were rows upon rows of slot machines standing to attention like military guardsmen and punters playing half a dozen machines at a time, all anxious to give their money away to the establishment as fast as possible. At the rear of this huge room was the entrance to the theatre. I marched up to the main man, oblivious to the thousand eyes watching my every move.

"Excuse me, could you tell me where to get in to see the show?" I enquired politely in my best British accent.

"Have you got your tickets, sir?" he replied.

"No," I said, quite matter-of-factly.

"Do you see all those people?" he said, pointing to a throng of people six deep in a queue that faded out of sight into the distance.

"Well, they all wanna see the show and they ain't got tickets either and they've all been here for hours."

I looked at the crowd, looked back at this imposing figure in his immaculately cut uniform and said quietly:

"You're trying to tell me something, aren't you?"

At this he just burst out laughing and said:

"I like your British style, come on in," and much to the chagrin of the waiting crowd he escorted us into the packed auditorium. It was a fine sight, jewellery rattling everywhere, pearly teeth flashing on all sides and opulence streaming from all corners.

"Table for two," I said confidently to the flunky who looked at me inquiringly.

"You'll have to share," he said.

I feigned a look of slight annoyance at the prospect of sharing, as though it wasn't really what we were used to, and agreed, in a most accommodating voice, just as though I was helping him out of a tricky situation.

"Down the middle, second table on the left," he commanded, and we marched down the aisle. Any table in this area was going to be superb, an uninterrupted view, almost as good as being up there on stage with Frank.

Sure enough, two spare seats on the second table on the left; each table seated three on each side and the other seat on our table was already occupied by one of the most famous bald heads in the world.

"Sit down, pussycats," he said, and we made ourselves comfortable for an evening with 'Kojak'. Telly Savalas was charm personified as we enjoyed a super performance by 'The Guv'nor' up on the stage. We hadn't paid to get in and Telly insisted on paying for all our wine and goodies. As well as being one of the best evenings of my life it was also the cheapest.

I was feeling quite euphoric as Frank finished his act with numerous curtain calls and, quite out of character for me, I announced to Peter that we should complete the evening by meeting the man himself. His security arrangements and his minders were legendary throughout the world, but that never entered my head as I ambled backstage in search of Francis Albert.

I didn't have far to look because there he was, seated at a table with his wife. Strategically placed on all four sides were the biggest gorillas I have ever seen, bursting out of their tuxedos. I decided to approach the one that looked almost human, and he told me that I would have to speak to his famous manager, Gilly Rizzo, if I wanted to see Francis.

He was seated a few feet away just about to tuck into a giant steak. I decided I didn't have time to mess about or bother with any niceties. So I spoke to Gilly in the same manner in which I imagined he spoke to everybody else. He was a short, thick-set, squat man, with a mean face and horn-rimmed glasses. I'm sure he had ordered many a dreadful deed to be carried out on any poor wretch who had happened to displease him in the past, but I was in the mood for anything as I yelled across to him:

"Gilly. I haven't got time to mess about, take us over to Frank because I'm in a rush."

He looked up in amazement, and said:

"Oh, sure, sorry to have kept you," put his knife and fork down, pushed past a few people and hurried over.

"Sorry about that," he said.

Even I didn't know what was going on now. Does he think I'm Prince Charles or something?

"Anyone who's a pal of Joe Louis's is a pal of mine," he said to me as we approached Frank.

Joe Louis, 'The Brown Bomber', former Heavyweight Champion of the world, was now a sick man and worked as a 'greeter' at Caesar's. How he entered the proceedings at this point I will never know, but I was grateful to him.

"Frank, this guy's from England, a buddy of Joe's," he said, as he graciously pulled out a chair for me to sit down on.

I spent an entertaining ten minutes with Frank, hoping Joe Louis wouldn't appear at any moment. I sampled his vino, had an interesting chat, and then bade him a fond farewell before my luck ran out. As I made my way to the exit I saw a huge one-armed bandit, the biggest in the world. I've never gambled on anything in my life, except myself, but said to Peter:

"With the sort of night we've had, stick a five-dollar piece in."

We would have done anything that night. The noise was deafening as the jackpot clanged down into the huge bucket at the foot of the machine, and with that we were off, into the Nevada evening air.

Some people have all the luck.

Games in Canada followed, one in the shadow of the amazing Niagara Falls, about 90 miles from Toronto, and another in Kitchener, Ontario, where we played the Canadian national team. In this game I converted my usual penalty and also collected a lovely 'Man of the Match' trophy that was not quite so usual for me.

Australia
(The Galloping Major)

Kevan Walsh had been a young apprentice with me at Maine Road many years ago, having blazed the trail from Australia for a trial, long before Craig Johnston or Mark Viduka were even born, in the hope of making a career in football for himself, just like his dad Billy, who is one of Manchester City's most revered former international players.

Billy Walsh actually represented four different countries at international level during his long, illustrious career. Two years playing for England Schoolboys, caps for both Northern Ireland and the Republic of Ireland and finally international recognition for New Zealand in the twilight of his playing days. His most memorable international was in 1949 when he inspired the Republic of Ireland to their most famous victory, beating England 2–0 at Goodison Park. England, with Billy

Wright and Neil Franklin in defence and Tom Finney and Wilf Mannion in attack, were tipped to win by an embarrassingly huge score-line but with Walsh prompting and probing from the right-half position, Ireland produced one of the biggest shocks of all time by ending the game as comfortable winners.

Kevan had inherited some of his dad's talent but not enough of it and it was a sad day for us both when the club did not renew his contract. After a brief spell in London he returned home down under and became a famous pop star. As you do.

We had become close friends. We had played together, struggled together, moaned together, hit Butlins Pwllheli together, and as I finally waved him goodbye on the day that he left England for good, we vowed to stay in touch. And we did, because over 30 years later it was a lovely surprise to receive a letter bearing an Australian post mark inviting Judith and I to travel halfway round the world to stay with him and his wife Sue at their home in Melbourne. It was an invitation we couldn't and didn't refuse, and we had a marvellous time in the Australian sunshine.

Kevan was now a teacher, quite a contrast to his earlier hectic lifestyle on the road as a member of the pop group The Pleasers. They had become quite famous, toured with other top-name bands like The Dave Clark Five and generally had a rock 'n' rolling good time. But now with the love of Sue, he had settled quite easily into a more tranquil way of life, illustrated perfectly by the idyllic day we spent in the Dandenong Mountains on the outskirts of the city.

"There's a big game on tonight, Fred."

Kevan mentioned it casually, almost as an afterthought, obviously not realising that I had already been suffering severe withdrawal symptoms since the end of the football season a mere three weeks previously. The prospect of watching a game in Australia that very evening sounded particularly appealing.

"The best team in Melbourne against the best team in Sydney," said Kev. "Most of the Australian national team will be playing and I think I can get tickets."

An hour later, we were parking the car and walking towards the ground. Fantastic. It doesn't matter where you are in the world; the feeling is just the same. Floodlights streaming down, crowds walking expectantly towards the turnstiles, excited kids chattering away to their dad, running alongside him just to keep up. Programme sellers, fast-food stalls, souvenir stalls, everything that goes together to make a big game something special. There was just half an hour to go before kick-off, and our tickets were waiting for collection at reception, courtesy of Bobby McLoughlin, an exiled Scot then managing a rival Melbourne club.

"G'd evening gentlemen, enjoy the game," said the commissionaire, and we were in.

The ground of South Melbourne Hellas Soccer Club was small and compact; nicely maintained and heavily sponsored, exclusively so, it seemed, by companies specialising in food. 'Kapiris Bros' for fruit, 'Dodoni' for cheese, 'Stragos Catering' and main sponsors 'Marathon Foods'. Nobody would ever starve at this club.

"The directors' box is on the other side of the ground, so we'll have to walk round," said Kevan, and as we weaved our way through the crowd, watching the players from both teams limbering up at each end of the pitch, I could see a photographer in the centre circle waving frantically in our direction.

"Kev, that photographer's waving at you," I said.

Kev looked a little bemused, but being a nice fellow, waved vaguely back in his direction although he obviously had no idea who he was. The photographer shook his head, kept waving and pointing, and finally beckoned me to climb over the perimeter wall and join him in the centre circle.

"He means you," said Kevan.

"He can't mean me," I replied. "Not in Australia."

I looked over my shoulder to check if there was anybody behind me. No, he meant me. So I cocked my leg over the wall and seconds later, I was standing in the centre circle under the floodlights, surrounded by Australia's finest, discussing the old days at Manchester City with a photographer from Wythenshawe who used to bunk off from school to watch us all train at Maine Road. Amazing really, and by this time, I was really beginning to feel at home. The atmosphere was great and I was in no hurry to leave the pitch as we wandered about chatting, in between him taking photographs of the players and me dying to have a kick of one of the balls.

Eventually we found ourselves in the top half of the pitch where the home team was warming up, and strolling among them was an elderly, portly-looking gent, a cross between Alfred Hitchcock and Robert Morley.

He was wearing a short-sleeved sports shirt pulled tightly over an enormous waistline, beige slacks, and he had tiny feet encased in a pair of light brown slip-on moccasin shoes.

The whole ensemble was topped off with what I thought were quite a trendy pair of shades for an old man, but I gave him no more than a cursory glance until a stray ball rolled invitingly into his path.

Now, I am not sure just how much of the ball he could actually see over his pot-belly, but in one movement the left moccasin flicked the ball up into the air and volleyed it with unerring accuracy into the top corner of the net. The keeper just simply stood and watched it fly in. A truly magnificent effort.

"Go and get a contract quick and get the old guy signed up," I said jokingly to my new best photographer friend.

"Ah yes," he replied with a little smile. "Mister Puskas, he's still the best striker of a ball that I have ever seen."

Mister Puskas?

MISTER PUSKAS ... Bloody hell, PUSKAS ... FERENC PUSKAS, THE GALLOPING MAJOR. Kocsis, Hidegkuti and Puskas, Gento, Di Stefano and Puskas. It is him, I couldn't believe it. I admit it, I stood transfixed, I was on the same pitch as Ferenc Puskas. Okay, he was sixty-four years old, but who cares. I could tell him everything he might want to know about himself, anything he might want to know about his fantastic Hungarian team that had beaten England so comprehensively in 1953, or of his Honved team that had played against Wolverhampton Wanderers in those famous early floodlight games at Molyneux in 1954. Real Madrid *v* Eintracht at Hampden Park, what a game of football that was. And years before that how my dad and I had stood and waited for hours just to see him play for Real Madrid against Manchester United. Now here he was in far-off Australia, no more than a neat side-footed pass away from me and as I looked at him, I thought, 'THAT, my legendary Hungarian friend, is exactly what you are going to get any minute now,' because I knew that if I remained where I was for a few more precious moments, a wayward pass would find its way to me and here in Middle Park, Melbourne, where it had once been Boggart Hole Clough in Blackley, I would be the little football-mad kid with the red hair and freckles again.

Raymond Glendenning takes up the commentary:

> The ball runs loose to Eyre in midfield, not many players could have controlled a tricky bounce like that, but Eyre is not just any player. He looks up and picks out Puskas with a glorious through pass of such quality that the Hungarian captain only has to tap the ball into the net with his famous left foot.

Germany 0, The Rest of the World 1

I was snapped back into life by an Australian voice shouting for me to knock back to him the ball that was heading my way. He looked good, Trimboli, the Aussie international, star player, tall, slim, athletic, even suntan glistening with oil on his toned legs in the evening sunshine, engaging smile, his arms and the palms of his hands outstretched in an invitation to simply pass him his ball back. No Chance. Not an earthly. There is only one place that this ball is going. There is only one person that this pass is going to and with one deft touch the ball is under control.

'Not many players could have controlled a tricky bounce like that.'

I have to say at this point, I was a little disappointed at the great man's vision because when I looked up,

'To pick him out with a glorious through pass ... '

he was actually looking the other way with his hands thrust deeply inside the pockets of his beige slacks. Not quite what I had in mind.

Then came the master stroke, a touch of genius, a lifetime of playing, studying and reading about the game all came together in the next glorious second.

"OCSI!" I shouted.

This was the nickname given to him as a schoolboy some sixty years previously in Kispest, the tiny village on the outskirts of Budapest where he was brought up. To quote Michael Caine, 'Not a lot of people know that.' But I did, and the reaction was instant. He spun round, the look of astonishment on his face was quickly replaced by one of concentration as I fired a peach of a pass straight at him and moved off quickly to let him know that I expected an equally good one in return. Sure enough, here it was, nicely weighted, into my path and I took it in my stride. I was tempted to shoot and put 'The Rest of the World' into the lead myself, but that wouldn't have been right, so very unselfishly I knocked it to him again for the old left foot to sizzle another one into the roof of the net from just outside the box. By this time both sets of players were drifting off the pitch towards the dressing-rooms to prepare for the actual game. As if I cared, as Puskas and I walked off arm in arm.

Final Score: Germany 0, The Rest of the World 1

TWENTY-NINE

A Man of Property

BACK HOME, I THOUGHT MY FOOTBALL 'CAREER' WAS winding down and I deliberately signed to play in a lower league than I had been used to, simply to enjoy a final fling. I could help any player in the team who appreciated a bit of help, would be able to enjoy my game, giving it everything I'd got for the 90 minutes of course, but with no real pressures.

I signed for the well-known amateur side Northern Nomads where Brooky had played for fifteen years man and beast, and renewed my full-back partnership with him. But only after a scare from the manager, Doug Walker, an ex-Manchester City goalkeeping colleague of mine. Before the season started he said to me:

"Come along for training and we'll try and sort something out for you."

Brooky was with me at the time and as Doug drove off in his car I said:

"God, it must be some team you've got here, if he might only be able to sort something out for me."

Sure enough, I only made an appearance as a substitute in the first pre-season friendly game. Thankfully that was enough to prove to Doug that I was up to the required standard and I was never left out of the team the whole time I was there; but in a way, I even had to have a trial to sign for Northern Nomads.

Doug Walker was a huge asset to the club and I really enjoyed playing for him. I had a super time as a Nomad. With my past record it was fitting that I signed for them at some time. When I turned up for that first game, there were two other 'trialists' there; both of them were actually young enough to be my sons.

One was a tricky little left-winger with a bright personality called Garry Kirkwood, a lovely kid who entertained me on and off the pitch with his japes and good humour, but infuriated me on it when his tricks didn't quite come off. I, the old man playing directly behind him, had to constantly sweat blood to retrieve a situation, while he looked on with his cheeky young face glowing with the innocence of youth.

The other one was a different proposition altogether. Quiet, but not missing anything, respectful, but not too much, with a mop of floppy hair. He looked a bit small to be a centre-forward, but there was a cool air of determination about him that I immediately liked.

I liked him even more once the game had kicked off and I received a short throw-out from our goalkeeper, wide on the left. I took one touch onto my left foot and looked up fully expecting, as usual, to see the numbers 10 and 9 on the backs of the strikers' shirts as they raced away like headless chickens towards the goal, expecting me to drop a Johnny Haynes-style pass into their path without them even having to break their stride.

Of course the ball never got there, but this was the normal procedure at this level of football. But not today, not with this lad. I looked up and there he was in acres of space, facing me, demanding the ball. He looked as big as a barn door as I picked him out with a raking pass. I couldn't miss him.

"Mmm, not bad," I thought as he controlled it on his chest, laid it off in one movement, turned and galloped into the penalty area for the return pass that obviously never came. Perfect centre-forward play.

This went on throughout the entire 90 minutes. He was a joy to play with and at the end of the game Doug asked all three of us to sign, but I knew that the centre-forward Craig Madden would not be with us for long. He was destined for much better things. I sent him down to Bob Smith at Bury and his record of 129 goals for 'The Shakers' is going to take some beating.

Doug was a very intelligent and successful businessman and his work was encroaching into his football. I felt sure he was going to resign before long, so when I received an offer from another ex-colleague, David Wild, to sign for Chadderton, I did so and Brooky came along with me.

If I had thought Doug Walker was going to remain manager I would have stayed with him, but he did in fact retire shortly afterwards.

It was certainly 'interesting' at Chadderton. There were times when David wasn't at the games, through illness, working or scouting, and on those occasions I was put in charge of the team as a player-deputy manager. Being a player-manager is one of the hardest jobs in the world. It's not easy to stand shivering in your muddy kit at half-time, attempting to put right what went wrong in the first half when inwardly you know that you were one of the major problems.

Despite that, I felt comfortable in the role. I spoke to each player in turn, told him what I thought his failings were, told him what I thought his strengths were, and that we were all going to play to each other's strengths and play around the weaknesses. The response from the players on each occasion was tremendous, and I never had any trouble, even from players who were renowned for being difficult. David was always appreciative of my efforts and used to discuss everything with me.

Except, of course, the time he decided to leave me out of the team. It was a freezing cold day, but it was lovely and warm in my car so I decided to go in my shirt-sleeves to the match. The two strides from the car to the warm dressing-room was the only time I would be subjected to the cold, so I assumed I would be okay. I thought David gave me a rather sheepish look when I arrived, but I didn't pay too much attention as I entered the dressing-room. He then gave me the usual immortal words:

"You've been playing well but I want to see how the younger players do with a view to next season."

"Okay," I replied.

I said I couldn't stay and watch the game even though I wanted to because I was only in my shirt-sleeves and it was so cold I had just seen a brass monkey with a blow lamp looking for a welder. He said he understood and so I drove away from the ground, little knowing I would never return.

The following day I received a call from Wigan Athletic. Harry McNally, the manager from my Chorley days, was now the manager of the reserve team at Wigan. They were a young side and needed an old head like mine to help them along. Would I like to join them?

It was a great move for me. Wigan Athletic were the cream

of non-league football. Their ground, Springfield Park, was at the time superior to many league grounds, and compared to the slag heaps I had been playing on recently it seemed like Wembley to me. The job Harry wanted me to do really appealed, but even though I had felt a little hard done to the day before, I still felt a loyalty towards David Wild.

Harry wanted me to play on Tuesday evening. I said I would let him know after telephoning David Wild to put him in the picture and discuss the situation. I didn't have to telephone David, because later that day he rang me.

"Do you want to play in the reserves on Tuesday?" he said.

Chadderton Reserves versus Irlam Town Reserves was not a fixture that really gripped my imagination but being a 'good pro' I wanted to set a good example and let everybody know that Fred Eyre was not too much of a big-time Charlie not to accept being relegated to the reserve team. So I would definitely have been, under normal circumstances, prepared to play.

The FA Rules stated that a player could play in both of the two totally unconnected leagues that Chadderton and Wigan Athletic Reserves played in, without transferring the player's registration, so I could play for both teams without any fuss.

I said to David:

"If it's the reserve team I'd rather not."

I was going to go on and tell him about Wigan Athletic and how flattered I was that they had showed interest in an old lag like me and could I, if he did not object, go over and see them on Tuesday evening instead. But he simply slammed the phone down in mid-sentence and I never saw or spoke to him again. I still attended his funeral a few years later, after he sadly died at quite a young age. We were team-mates for too long for me not to be very, very sad.

With this small question of my loyalty to David now apparently answered, I drove over to Wigan to enter yet another interesting phase of my life. I arrived at Springfield Park, as with all my other matches, in very good time, swung the gleaming Rolls into the car park, but did not get out. All of a sudden I got a feeling that I had never had before. I felt very old. I simply could not bring myself to enter the ground and I just sat there in the car and listened to the radio. Soon, young kids began to arrive, clutching Tesco bags which presumably contained their boots. Each lad seemed to be dressed the same—faded jeans, Adidas training shoes, and donkey jacket. I heard one young player remark:

"The referee must be worth a few bob," as he pointed to me in my car.

Little did he know that in half an hour he would be lining up alongside me. I still didn't move. I just didn't want to go through the door. Just like that time at Bradford. Here I was, a successful businessman, veteran of 1,000 games, who'd travelled the world, and I was reticent about going into the dressing-room at Wigan Athletic.

Eventually I could leave it no longer. As with all match days, I was dressed in a smart suit, shirt and tie, just the opposite of my team-mates. As the away-team coach arrived at the ground, I walked in with them, but when we got through the door, they all turned right and I turned left into the door marked 'Home Team'. What a performance just to enter the ground; hard to imagine that a couple of years later I would be appointed manager of the club.

I was having an Indian summer, and I wanted it to last for ever. I gained the respect of the kids. They did what I asked and I carried Harry's instructions out onto the field to the letter. Life was dealing me a good hand to finish off my career and I was loving every minute of it.

It helped that in front of me on the left-hand side of midfield was a player who looked as though he had been around the block a few times. He was tough, he tackled anything that moved, and he looked after me like he would have looked after his old granddad. He protected me, did most of my running for me and generally cosseted me from all those nasty opponents, who game after game seemed intent on running the ancient legs off me. It was a nice feeling. Usually, it was the other way round, but I felt quite content having my own personal 'minder' close to me for 90 minutes twice a week.

Danny Wilson looked and played like he was about 28, but talked and dressed like a 48 year old. He was a very good player, and one who I would definitely have recommended to Bob at Bury again if he had been a bit younger, but I thought he was far too old.

Nelson away on a Tuesday night between Boxing Day and New Year is not really a fixture for the soccer purists, but we had won and I had played well. Danny had played magnificently in front of me, but I was feeling a little bit morose. I sat alone at the front of the old coach, smoke bellowing out of the exhaust as the engine ticked over. It was 10.30 on a freezing cold night and we were waiting for the directors to finish their drinks in the little boardroom, so that we could all get off home.

I was sad because in the Nelson team had been my great friend Ken Bracewell from my days at Lincoln City, 'Remember, Fred, when the dressing-room door closes' etc. He was recovering from a badly broken leg, but such was his love of the game that, even with his obvious discomfort and the fact that he was now 41 years of age, he was still 'giving it one last go'. What a guy, and what a friend to me. I sincerely hoped that it wasn't to be 'the factory door' for him, as he had predicted all those years ago.

"Fred, we're all going out after training on Thursday, are you coming with us?"

It was Danny from the back of the bus. How sweet, I thought, not leaving the old man out but secretly hoping that I would say no, so I wouldn't cramp their style down at Cassenelli's.

"Naw, thanks anyway but I'll give it a miss," I shouted back over my shoulder.

Strangely, on this occasion Danny wouldn't take 'Naw' for an answer and he tried to smooth-talk me.

"Come on, you miserable old sod, it's my birthday on New Year's Day, a triple celebration — the New Year, my birthday and the fact that I can now start learning to drive. You've got to come."

I turned round in disbelief.

"Learn to drive? Are you telling me that you are only 16 years of age?"

I was looking at the oldest teenager in captivity.

"Seventeen on the first of January," he said, rubbing his hands together gleefully.

I changed my mind and promised to be there, but before

that I had another little phone call to make, and before long Danny Wilson was also on his way to Bob at Gigg Lane.

Not a bad few months in the history of Bury Football Club. Two players signed for nothing who would eventually be worth hundreds of thousands of pounds between them during their brilliant careers, and all because Bob and I used to play football together as kids in Boggart Hole Clough.

Football, however, has a way of knocking the legs from under you. Two weeks later the directors of Wigan Athletic Football Club announced that they were disbanding their reserve team 'for financial reasons', so a host of talented young players were released. Harry McNally was out of a job and I was out to grass; should I finally call it a day and concentrate on my business, which had thankfully continued to prosper?

• • •

The shop in Princess Street was doing well and I thought I was set there for life, until a tall, distinguished-looking gentleman came into the shop one lunch-time. He walked through the door, ignored the counter, which is where most customers head for, but instead looked round the whole shop, up into the corners, his eyes missing nothing as he surveyed the entire scene. I stood and watched him, quietly amused at this unusual situation. I became slightly less amused when he wandered down to our private quarters at the rear of the shop, still casting a professional eye over every little thing.

"Can I help you?" I enquired, trying desperately to conceal my anger.

"No, it's all right," he replied casually, still eyeing up the place.

"I'm afraid it's not all right," I corrected him. "I own this shop and this department is not accessible to the public."

"My clients are contemplating buying this building and I need to inform them what they are getting for their money."

At this point two things happened. Firstly I slung the man out of the shop and secondly I decided there and then to move. I have always tried to be decisive but I was at my best on this occasion. I arrived home that evening and as I tucked into my evening meal, I informed Judith, quite calmly, that Fred Eyre Stationers would be moving.

"Where to?" was her obvious first question.

I had to admit that I hadn't a clue, but we would definitely be moving, and furthermore, this time when we did move I would own the building. There would never be an occasion again when a total stranger would walk through the door and announce a change of landlord. From this day on I would be my own landlord. I don't know who the gentleman was but his visit that day did me the biggest favour possible. It made me think of something that had simply never entered my head before. I would buy my own building and become a man of property.

As in the past, I thought Sunday would be the best day to begin my search and I went through the same ritual as I had before in search of premises, only this time my sights were set a little higher.

After much searching, my mind kept coming back to a building on John Dalton Street, a quality business street about 50 yards from my present position. It looked an ideal building, with six floors, including a shop, ample office space and plenty of much-needed storage space for stock. I thought it would suit my purposes admirably. The only problem was that it wasn't for sale. The shop was 'To Let' and so were each of the individual offices, but I thought it was expecting a lot for each unit to be let individually so I decided to jump straight in and offer a price to buy the lot.

It was a pretty bold step for a Blackley boy to take. It meant a few hardships. Our holiday house in Anglesey, bought as an investment in partnership with Brooky, had to be sold, a bit of belt tightening here and there, but nothing too drastic. The lovely house in Worsley that I had bought for my parents so they could be near to us had been paid for in full. I owned every brick of that, so that was no problem. It was one of my greatest thrills to see them so nicely settled in a house of their own with no worries, and I wouldn't have done anything to jeopardise that.

I managed to clinch the deal and a matter of weeks later I became the owner of a complete six-storey building in the city centre of Manchester. I set about refurbishing the place to my own specification. As with my previous premises, there were only three of us left there as we finally locked up in the early hours, my preparations completed for the big opening six hours later. My mother and father had stayed the course with me until the last nail was knocked in.

. . .

Harry McNally, meanwhile, had been appointed assistant manager at Southport Football Club in the Fourth Division of the Football League.

Southport had been struggling for many seasons and often

had to apply for re-election to the league at the end of the season. Now they had appointed a new management team of Hughie Fisher as player-manager and Harry McNally as his assistant.

I thought this a sensible appointment because Hughie Fisher had been, and indeed still was, a very good player. Having begun his career at Blackpool he moved on to Southampton, where he held down a first-team place for many seasons, and was substitute in the 1976 Cup final when Southampton surprisingly beat Manchester United 1–0 at Wembley with a goal from Bobby Stokes.

Now he felt ready to move into management but, having always dealt with the level of player that was out of the reach of Southport, it was felt he needed the assistance of a man who knew the lower regions of the game inside out. Such a man was Harry McNally.

Harry proved his shrewdness again by signing me for Southport. So at an age when most players are thinking of taking up tiddlywinks or chess, I found myself back with a Football League club again. He wanted me to do the job with the kids I had done before, and of course I was happy to do it.

Occasionally my two lives overlapped. For one evening fixture away at Bradford City in midweek I decided to travel to Valley Parade by car and meet up with the other players at the ground. They, of course, had travelled by coach, but this arrangement enabled me to work in the shop all day, before locking up at 5.30. It was a dark, horrible midwinter night as I drove over the Pennines with that day's takings in the boot of my car, and as I crawled my way through one of Bradford's less salubrious areas, I suddenly began to feel a trifle uneasy at the prospect of playing 90 minutes' football with a stash of money nestling alongside my spare wheel in the car park. I turned into Manningham Lane and decided to take the cash into the dressing-room with me, but as I changed into my kit and saw the number of different characters traipsing in and out before the game, it dawned upon me that maybe that wasn't such a good idea either.

Goalkeeper John Coates solved the problem for me, by hiding it in his cap and casually slinging it into the corner of his netting, the way that all keepers do, and that was where it remained for the full 90 minutes. Needless to say, I always defended that particular goalpost for corners during that game. I was embarking upon another very happy period. I loved my time at Southport.

I was on holiday in Cornwall when I heard the sad news. I switched on the television in the hotel just in time to hear that Southport Football Club had finally lost its league status and its place in the Football League was to be taken by Wigan Athletic.

This short, simple statement meant nothing but sorrow to me at that moment, but it was to be a very significant moment for me as far as my football career was concerned.

THIRTY

Wigan Athletic Football Club

WIGAN ATHLETIC'S ACCEPTANCE INTO THE FOOTBALL League, after many unsuccessful applications, meant a complete reappraisal of everything at Springfield Park. Firstly, all concerned had to change from part time to full time — the manager, the secretary, the groundsman and, of course, the players. This was not as easy and straightforward as it sounds. Many players had reached a stage in their jobs where they were simply too old to change their occupations. They were good enough to play in the Fourth Division, no question, but having attained a certain level in their working lives, thought it unwise for them to throw it all away for the glamour of being a full-time professional footballer for a couple of seasons.

It was also felt that the now-defunct reserve team should be resurrected and with this in mind, keeper Phil Critchley suggested to manager Ian McNiell that I would be ideal for the job of running it. I always knew Phil was a good goal-keeper, but hadn't realised that he possessed such perception. It also says much for Mr McNiell that he felt confident enough to give me the chance.

I accepted the job, never mentioning whether or not I was to be paid. I also asked for and was given Brooky as my right-hand man, even though Mr McNiell had other, more experienced pros in mind for the job. This was the first instance where Ian McNiell showed his qualities as a leader by giving me the job and giving me the man I wanted alongside me. From that moment on he never interfered with the way I tackled the job.

I like to think, of course, that I never gave him any cause to worry. I'm sure if I had done anything to displease him he would have straightened me out, but the fact remained that he left me completely alone to do the job, and I presume, in view of that, that I must have done it to his satisfaction.

I know that we were extremely pleased to have him as our boss. Both Brooky and I had the utmost respect for him. He was a fine man, a super person, who always stood by us, and did a great job for Wigan Athletic while he was the manager. It was a sad day in the Eyre and Brooks households when two and a half seasons later we learned that he was to lose his job.

Our brief at the outset was, quite simply, to get a team onto the field for the first game against Blackpool. The boss had problems of his own; he had about eight weeks to turn the whole club into a full-time set-up. We had about four weeks to sift through the many trialists to find a team from scratch to compete at the same level as the youngsters of Manchester United, City, Liverpool, Everton and the rest.

I set myself a list of rules that I intended to follow the whole time I was in football management at whatever level it might be. Up to now I have found no cause to stray from them.

I had encountered so many bad managers and coaches during my career that if I treated my players the exact opposite to the way I had been treated, I knew I would be on the right lines.

Be honest. I can't see any reason for telling lies to players.

Be organised. Know exactly what you are going to do in training, know exactly what you want in matches and know exactly what you are going to say when certain situations crop up.

This, together with my basic knowledge of the game and my memory for players from yesteryear and the present day, has stood me in good stead in dealing with players of all ages and temperaments.

My favourite species in football is 'The Good Pro'. There is nothing I admire more in soccer than a good professional. After taking charge of the reserve team at Wigan it was a pleasure to team up with some who I held in very high regard.

I was perhaps fortunate that the first of these was Micky Worswick, a tremendous favourite with the Springfield Park fans for many years. Micky was in the Wigan Athletic team when it was elected to the league but felt he was a little too old to turn full time. His attitude and application set the trend for the rest of the players and not one of them ever let me down, despite the obvious disappointment of not being in the first team where they felt they belonged.

From the minute I arrived at Springfield Park as a coach, I felt completely at home. I really loved the place, a feeling I had not really known since my days at Maine Road. I felt it a little at Chorley, a little at Rossendale, both nice homely clubs, but I had a special feeling at Springfield Park.

The main reason was the manager, but the secretary, Derek Welsby, also went out of his way to help me and make me feel at home. Ronnie Pye made life easier for me on training nights, providing us with good facilities. The chairman and directors were polite and treated me as a member of the staff, which of course I was, but only part time after all. Even though Brooky and I were constantly aware of this, it seemed to make no difference to the directors who always treated us with respect. In fact everybody was really kind. Except for the door man. This gentleman, who manned the main entrance on match days, really put Brooky and I in our place when we arrived for the first home game of the season. We both turned up together, and parked our beautiful cars in the deserted car park, because as usual we had arrived extra early. The sun was shining as we strolled together towards the official players' entrance, thinking how smart we looked in our best suits, shirts and ties, everything that two smart young coaches should be wearing on match days.

"Good afternoon," we greeted the steward cheerfully as we side-stepped him to go through the narrow door.

"You can't come in here," he growled, as he moved across to completely block the door.

"Why not?" we enquired, trying not to look too put out.

"The caterers go in through the entrance further down," he replied, which really took the wind out of our sails.

"Do we look like the men who deliver the pies?"

Still, this was only a minor irritation and nothing, not even the steward, could dampen our spirits as we set to work for our new club.

The first season in the Football League was a huge success for Wigan Athletic. They finished a highly respectable sixth in the league, and my reserve side finished a little higher in our league, so it was a good season for both teams. The directors rewarded this with a holiday in Majorca, a gesture that was really appreciated by all the players and even more so by Brooky and myself, who were also invited along at the insistence of Mr McNiell. The directors originally suggested a round-the-world cruise, but the players wanted to go somewhere else!

The second season things went even better. The first team finished in sixth place again and my team ended up even higher than it did the previous season. This was coupled with a good Cup run when we disposed of Blackpool and Northwich Victoria, both after replays, and a memorable victory at Stamford Bridge when a Tommy Gore chip was enough to eliminate the famous Chelsea 1–0 and put Wigan into the hat for a tremendous fixture away at Everton.

Goodison Park was crammed with 52,000 people, the biggest gate of the season. About 20,000 were from Wigan, all hoping to see 'Latics perform one of the biggest giant-killing acts of all time. Unfortunately they were to be disappointed, not in the performance of the team, but in the result. Goals from Joe McBride, Brian Kidd and Bob Latchford gave the Toffeemen a 3–0 victory, but this still did nothing to diminish another fine season, and again the directors sent us off on holiday, this time to sunny Malta for a week's rest at the top hotel on the island.

Trips abroad like this, continual ground improvements, good performances on the field, a youth policy that was paying dividends in unearthing, developing and producing its own young players, first-class travel to games, best hotel accommodation, all of these things went together to make people inside football sit up and take notice. Here was a football club that did things in the correct manner, a club that was going places, a club of substance and, above all, a club with great potential.

This potential was recognised by the shrewd eye of Mr Freddie Pye, chairman of Stockport County, who I feel must have looked at the set-up at Springfield Park and compared it to his own at Edgeley Park. His shrewd eye became an envious one. Although comparative infants to league football, the difference between the two clubs was vast and Mr Pye saw more scope to achieve his ambition of being chairman of a successful football club at Wigan than there was at Stockport County.

Freddie Pye is a self-made man, a Stockport lad who wanted to be a professional footballer but who never quite made the top grade, and graced the lower regions, playing for a number of clubs in the Cheshire League and the Welsh League. This story sounds a little familiar.

He thought that if he was going to end up on the scrapheap at least he should own it. He opened a number of scrap-metal yards in and around the Manchester area, and secured his business future. At the same time he was the successful manager of Altrincham when, under his guidance plus the drive and enthusiasm of Noel White and Peter Swales, who moved on to bigger and better things at Liverpool and Manchester City respectively, they put the hitherto unknown name of Altrincham Football Club on the map. So with his business acumen and his association with soccer, both as a player and a manager, he brought a little more knowledge to the position of chairman of Wigan Athletic than one would normally expect.

The present chairman, Mr Horrocks, became president of the club, a move which pleased me personally because I always felt that Mr Horrocks added a touch of dignity to the club, was proud to be part of Wigan Athletic and was a fine ambassador.

Mr Pye's first move was to invite onto the board England's number-one footballer for many years, the incomparable Bobby Charlton. His 106 caps, his never-to-be-forgotten goals, his impeccable behaviour on the field for Manchester United and England made him a legend throughout the world and now here he was with me at Wigan Athletic.

As far as Brooky and I were concerned the first bombshell of the new season came when Mr McNiell informed us that the club intended to withdraw us from the Lancashire League that had served us so well the previous two seasons and enter us in the newly formed Umbro Floodlit League.

This brought about my first ever conflict with the manager. The Umbro League operated only in midweek, which meant that except for the players on first-team duty, the whole of the Wigan Athletic playing staff was redundant every Saturday, traditionally the footballing day of the week.

Entering a midweek league almost completely cancelled out the midweek training sessions for the non-contract players whom I was responsible for, so the young players, who the club was relying on for its future, were to receive neither coaching nor fitness training.

If all of this wasn't bad enough, the league consisted of only five other teams. How anybody could contemplate even forming a league containing just six teams was beyond my comprehension, and when I was informed that we were to be one of the 'big six' I simply couldn't understand the reasoning behind it.

Some other clubs, I discovered, had remained in their various other leagues and were using the Umbro League as an auxiliary league to increase their number of games, but we were to be solely represented in this little league. I could only assume that the boss was not in possession of all the facts, so Brooky and I each took a morning off work to enlighten him, and we were confident that we could change his mind. We were wrong. The Umbro Floodlit League it was to be. My first thought and my second and third was to resign my position at the club.

This was something that I was really loath to do, but this simple, stubborn decision spelled disaster to me with a capital 'D'. The continuity of young players, which always takes a couple of years to get rolling, would now be broken and I knew it would be difficult to pick up the threads. I wouldn't be able to train and coach the players, which was something I felt I had proved I could do successfully, and I felt that their progress would be hampered by the lack of attention, so taking things all round I felt that there wasn't really a job left for me to do. It was only Dave Brooks' insistence that I gave it a go for the season that kept me at Wigan Athletic.

"Maybe the boss will realise his mistake by that time."

It gives me no pleasure to recall that he admitted to a serious error of judgement a long time before the season ended. By this time the damage had already been done. As far as I was concerned the reserve-team set-up, so good and professional and well organised in the past, simply spluttered along and eventually ground to a halt when we didn't play a single game for over two months. I felt it was all so unnecessary and self-destructive that during this period I confided in Dave Brooks that I definitely intended to 'jack the job in'. Again he dissuaded me.

"Wait a few more weeks, and then tell the boss that if we remain in this league next year we will be leaving," he suggested.

I agreed but didn't realise how many unlikely happenings would take place during those 'few more weeks'. There had been rumblings of discontent amongst the spectators for a number of weeks, as they watched the 'Latics stumble from game to game. They made it quite clear that they, the paying public, were far from satisfied with the team's performances this season. After the relative successes of the previous two seasons, they had hoped for something more in 1981 and when it became apparent that they were not going to get what they wanted, they singled out Ian McNiell as the target for their anger and frustration.

A little bit of barracking here and there on the terraces, one or two significant little asides in the newspapers, a few letters to the club, people sidling up to me in the town with knowing looks on their faces, each one forecasting the impending departure of the boss. Whenever this occurred I always made my feelings quite clear: we worked for him and we supported him. But the occasions when Brooky had to remove me from the ear bashings I was receiving from 'Latics fans were becoming more and more frequent.

It got so bad that I abandoned my usual practice of nipping into the social club for a drink after matches and chose instead to go straight home, rather than get involved in arguments supporting Ian McNiell. I could see, however, that the team was not responding on the field. After viewing an abysmal performance away to Port Vale, where we lost three-nil (to be honest we were lucky to get nil and they were unlucky not to get eight or nine), I remarked to my dad as we left the ground:

"I don't think the boss will survive this one," and unfortunately I was correct.

Monday 16th February was just like any other Monday at Fred Eyre Stationers until Freddie Pye rang and asked me to go and see him at his office. The thoughts in my mind as I drove to his office near Plymouth Grove were that the boss had been sacked, together with Kenny Banks and Ian Gillibrand, his two right-hand men at the club. I thought they must be dispensing with the entire staff in a clean sweep and that Brooky and I would go along with the rest.

'Thanks for everything in the past, please inform your mate Brooky,' and that would be that. Thank you and Goodnight Vienna. Still, we had done our best, until we were whipped out of the Lancashire League. I thought they were probably right. There wasn't really a job for us to do now and I was so fed up with the situation I was going to pack it in anyway, so I couldn't really blame them.

"Mr Eyre to see you, Mr Pye," said his secretary into the intercom.

I entered the chairman's large office, admired the many photographs of Fred with members of the Royal Family, Fred with some of the world's top sportsmen, but none of Fred with Frank Sinatra! He's got a long way to go.

I sat down and prepared myself for the news. I knew inwardly that he was going to tell me he had sacked the boss, but I wasn't really prepared for what came next.

"We would like you to take over as manager of Wigan

Athletic until we appoint a new man," he said.

I didn't want to be the manager of a football club and I remembered I hadn't enjoyed my last experience in this position. I suggested that if it was only to be until a new man was found, then why not say nothing to Mr McNiell and let him carry on until they found somebody. I was secretly hoping that if this were to happen, the team might start winning again and the crisis would be forgotten. Mr McNiell would never have known that there had been a problem and he would have kept his job. This suggestion was knocked back. It was felt that a change was necessary.

"What about Banksie or Gilly? They are full time and could keep things ticking over."

This was rejected out of hand. There was only me left, so after accepting the fact that there was nothing I could do to keep Mr McNiell in the job, I said that I would become manager of Wigan Athletic. I asked for Brooky to be my assistant again and when I approached him later in the day, he readily agreed. He couldn't start immediately, because he had to rearrange all his appointments, but would start as my right-hand man in about ten days' time.

My first day in charge gave me relatively few problems. The main one was in my own house. My son Steven, a staunch Ian McNiell fan, was so upset at the thought of him losing his job that I couldn't get him off to school.

Seeing Ian at the ground was also a bit of a tear-jerker for me, but a brief chat with him, a quick talk with the players, and a good light-hearted training session with them soon lifted the air of depression which hung over Springfield Park.

I decided not to make changes in the team simply for the

sake of it, but thought there was no point in selecting the same line-up as before. Something was obviously wrong, or Mr McNiell would still be in charge, so I decided to do the job, for whatever length of time, my own way and pick my own team. I would stand or fall by my own decisions, which is really all I have ever done.

The computer had thrown us a particularly hard fixture for my first game as manager. We were to play high-flying Mansfield Town at Springfield Park. 'The Stags' were placed third in the league, and although looking a good bet for promotion, couldn't afford to drop any points because there were a number of teams on their tail. I decided to be bold and decisive, and made seven changes from the squad who performed so badly the previous week at Port Vale. I was obviously hoping for a win, but also an improvement in attitude, application, will to win and a desire to help each other during the game. I also expected neatness and smartness in appearance when attending the game, a little thing that I felt had been sadly lacking. This was what I asked for and was exactly what I received from the players.

As I watched them leave the dressing-room I knew that if we were to lose this match it would only be because Mansfield were a great team and had beaten us by playing super football. I knew that if we were to lose it would not be for lack of effort. The crowd was understandably a little subdued at first, obviously wondering what this new unknown manager would be serving up for them, but when they saw the quality of football the players produced and the amount of honest sweat and toil they put in, they got right behind us and cheered us all the way to a wonderful 2–0 victory. There's nothing to this manager's job. All you have to do is win matches.

The following week moved along just as sweetly as the first; varied training sessions, something different each day to help to keep the players alert and keen, a new voice with fresh, bright, new ideas. This new approach helped them enjoy their training and soon Saturday was upon us again.

Another plum fixture, Bury away at Gigg Lane, a local derby. Our performance last week should ensure a good following for the short trip across Lancashire, plus the opportunity to see the 'Latics' former favourite Tommy Gore, my room-mate on the Malta and Majorcan jaunts, in action for his new club, having been transferred from Wigan earlier in the season following a number of little disagreements with Ian McNiell.

All in all the stage was set for a good afternoon as our coach weaved its way through the cobbled streets of Bury, about ten minutes away from Gigg Lane. It was a fairly quiet scene as players read the newspaper, played cards, or gazed idly out of the window at the shoppers in the busy Lancashire streets, some of them wearing Bury colours as they made their way to the ground.

"Put the radio on, driver, let's have a bit of music," came a voice from the back of the coach.

The driver clicked the switch and as if by remote control the announcer's voice blared out:

"Wigan Athletic have just announced that Nottingham Forest and England centre-half Larry Lloyd has been appointed their player-manager. He will commence his duties during the middle of next week."

I have never seen such looks of amazement on so many faces at one time; it seemed an eternity before anybody spoke. I must admit I was as shocked as the players. I had naively thought I might have been given the word before the media, so as not to be caught on the hop. It didn't upset me at all, because I knew I was only filling in until a new appointment was made, but to hear it on the team bus radio, five minutes before reaching the ground prior to an important fixture, was unfortunate to say the least. Still, we were stuck with the situation now and it was my job to get the minds of the players back on the job in hand, to beat Bury in three-quarters of an hour's time.

I pulled out all my old scripts to try and brighten up the dressing-room; if Brooky had been with me we could have performed our double act, but I was on my own. In fact, by the time he was ready to take up his appointment as my assistant, the job had gone, so he only nearly became an assistant manager.

A battery of photographers were at the players' tunnel as my team took the field, but unfortunately their cameras were not directed at them but at the directors' box, where Larry Lloyd was seated, having a preliminary look at the team that he was to inherit the following week. I hoped he wasn't going to be disappointed.

Again the players did not let me or themselves down and played with tremendous spirit and skill. I felt their performance warranted a little more than a 0–0 draw.

I was ready to hand over to Larry Lloyd with a record that should ensure me a place in the Guinness Book of Records as the only Football League manager never to lose a game, never to concede a goal in his entire management career, and still lose his job. I was hoping for half a bottle of whisky as a small consolation after being named 'Bell's Manager of the Fortnight'.

Larry Lloyd had enjoyed a glittering career. At 6ft 2ins he was a commanding figure at the heart of Liverpool's defence for several seasons. During his 150-game reign at Anfield he earned England Under-23 honours and in 1971 gained his first full international cap. He moved on to Coventry City, then Brian Clough took him to Nottingham Forest for a bargain £60,000 fee. In 1976 he helped Forest battle their way into the First Division. The following season he won League Championship and Football League Cup medals. The next two seasons he picked up two European Cup-winner's medals and also another England cap against Wales. Altogether, Larry had made over 400 league appearances and was now about to begin his managerial career at Wigan Athletic.

I was prepared to step back into the shadows, back to my reserve team, or even to step out altogether if Mr Lloyd wanted to bring in an entire new backroom staff. In the end Larry decided that even though he knew the game inside out, that his ideas were sound and that he was confident in his ability to manage and coach, he would benefit from the help of somebody who knew a little about life in the lower divisions, so he invited me to become his assistant manager.

I had never considered a life of full-time professional football ever since the game abandoned me when I was young and full of hopes and dreams. Now, at the age of 37, I was being offered a top position at a fine club like Wigan Athletic.

I decided to give myself the chance to put into practice all the things, good and bad, that I had picked up during my career by accepting the position as Larry Lloyd's right-hand man, only to find out that he was left-handed. Nevertheless, I pledged my support to him for one full season and immediately set about signing three solid hard-working professionals, who I knew would be the cornerstone of the promotion challenge together with the good players we had retained from the previous season.

John McMahon, a super right-back from Crewe, was the man I really wanted. I knew him to be just the right sort of character we needed for the job in hand and he came on a free transfer. Clive Evans and Graham Barrow came from Tranmere Rovers and Altrincham respectively and I was delighted with them both. Larry persuaded the old war-horse Les Bradd to sign for us from Stockport County. He proved to be one of the finest pros I have ever had the pleasure of working with and his combination up front with Mickey Quinn was simply too much for the Fourth Division to handle.

The goals they scored sent Wigan Athletic shooting into Division Three, but, true to form, by this time I was no longer with them.

THIRTY-ONE

Happy as Larry

WHOEVER COINED THAT PHRASE OBVIOUSLY DIDN'T consult me first, because while there were some lighter moments, life as Larry Lloyd's assistant was not one long barrel of laughs. It was like living on Mount Vesuvius, only sometimes a little more dangerous.

Our temperaments were a million miles apart and despite trying to convince myself that this mix of total opposites was the very ingredient that would make the chemistry work, I knew before the season was barely under way that I would be on my travels again pretty soon. I also knew that Larry's influence on the pitch was of enormous benefit to the players and there was no doubt in my mind that come the end of the season Wigan would win promotion, and that's exactly how things turned out. But with only a third of the season gone, the cracks between Larry and I were already beginning to show, and I began to spend less and less time in the office with him after training and more time in the dressing-room with the players, where I felt a little more comfortable and safe.

The players were resigned to Larry's wild outbursts. They had to be, really, because there was not a lot they could do about them. While it was a frightening sight to witness one of Larry's specials in full flight, they were beginning to happen so often that by this time they were making hardly any impact on the players at all.

We had already suffered the embarrassment of having to start the second half of a game against Bournemouth with only ten men because Larry had substituted two players at half-time. This, of course, was in the days when only one substitute was allowed. As soon as we reached the dressing-room at the end of the first-half, he banished strikers Tony and Mickey Quinn to the bath, after what he obviously considered to be a below-par performance from the pair of them. It was not until Larry and the nine other players were on the pitch that I nipped back into the dressing-room to fish Mickey out of the bath.

I helped him back into his kit and even though he was still dripping wet, I pushed him back onto the field, seven minutes into the second half, pausing only to give his thigh an imaginary final rub in an attempt to make the crowd think that I had been treating him for a pulled muscle. Harry Redknapp was the manager of Bournemouth then, and every time I have seen him since he has mentioned that game.

What was I going to do with Larry? The answer, of course, was nothing. He was the boss — strong-willed, single-minded, explosive and uncontrollable, except when chairman Freddie Pye was around. So if there were any adjustments to be made, I would have to be the one to make them. At first, because I was totally convinced that Wigan Athletic would win promotion that season, I thought that I might possibly be able to re-arrange my principles a little just long enough to help the club into the Third Division for the first time in their short Football League history.

It was a long time since I had come across such a complex character as Larry Lloyd. In our private moments I found him to be pleasant, if somewhat moody, company, but in front of the players it was a different matter and he never wasted a chance to give them a bit of stick.

There were occasional times, like our week's stay at Exeter University, when the mood needed lightening and he tried to become 'one of the lads' again by joining in the general banter. The players soon cottoned on to this and one player in particular used to make provocative remarks to the rest of the squad, in a voice just loud enough for Larry to hear as he strode by.

"He stayed out all last night you know."

"Who did?" demanded Larry.

"The man in the moon," the joker chortled as Larry took a deep breath and walked away.

A couple of days later, it was the same scene.

"He's definitely bent if you ask me."

"Who is?" said Larry.

"The man in the suitcase."

More chortling from the lads.

Larry summoned me to his room.

"Tell that Neil Davids to cut it out," he said. "I don't like it."

"Okay," I replied. "But it's only a bit of fun."

After dinner that evening, I spoke to the players and warned them of the dire consequences if the boss-baiting did not stop. They grumbled a bit, but agreed to be sensible.

A couple of days later the entire squad was dossing about watching the Test match in the television lounge, which was situated on the ground floor. Just as well, as things turned out. Larry came down the stairs looking immaculate in a full white tracksuit, with the Nottingham Forest emblem of a tree picked out in red on the breast. We had trained hard that morning. He had just come from the shower and in that European Cup-winning gear he looked the picture of health.

"What's the score?" he asked of nobody in particular.

All eyes remained glued to the screen as one of them piped up.

"He's one off 50."

I held my breath. No, surely not, they wouldn't dare. Right on cue Larry replied,

"Who is?"

Here it comes, I thought. It was like an Exocet missile—I could see it coming, but there was nothing I could do about it.

"PC49," Davids shrieked, as he jumped out of his chair, punched the air in delight and leapt through the window.

Larry gave me one of his looks and I shrugged my shoulders apologetically.

The end was not long in coming. Another home performance against league leaders Torquay United did not satisfy Larry, who proceeded to lambast his midfield players at the end of the game. They were the very three players whose extra efforts, in my opinion, had eventually managed to wrestle the game our way and had been the most influential in getting us a good result. I convinced myself that this roasting was nothing to do with me as I moved among the players, collecting the odd tie-up or shin-pad off the dressing-room floor. Most of them looked uncomfortable for the three lads who were taking the stick, because they knew they did not deserve it. One of them caught my eye as I busied myself with these imaginary jobs. He rolled his eyes up to his forehead and shook his head sadly as we waited for the storm to subside.

Finally the moment came. With the panache of a male stripper at a Thursday night hen party, he whipped off his jockstrap, threw it dramatically onto the dressing-room floor (which was a relief) and headed for the bathroom.

If that had been the end of the matter, yet another crisis would have been allowed to evaporate, like the steam now rising from the bath and Larry's ears. But as he drew level with me, I think even Larry must have been momentarily stunned by the deafening silence that had descended on a dressing-room that only minutes earlier had been bubbling with the excited chatter and noise of victory. He felt moved to enlist my support for his criticisms of the players concerned.

This was it. The moment that my credibility, my honesty and my character were put on the line. I had a fraction of a second to make up my mind which way to jump. I could feel the eyes of all the players upon me as Larry stood alongside me, totally naked, his huge sweaty shoulder level with my ear-hole, as we faced the whole dressing-room. I could see in the players' faces that they were mentally taking bets. Will he? Or won't he? They would all have understood if I had sided with the boss. This would have enabled me to join the long list of survivors, men who have stayed in the game all their lives at various clubs throughout the Football League simply by agreeing with the manager. I knew that Larry would never forgive me if I did not support him, because he had told me so within seconds of my appointment as his assistant six months earlier:

"Don't ever disagree with me in public. If you don't like something just swallow it and wait till we get back to the office."

I nodded in agreement at the time, thinking that it was a fair enough deal. Quite honestly, I thought that I would have no difficulty keeping my end of the bargain. I was wrong. There was no way that I could compromise myself in a situation like this, no matter how much I loved the job, no matter how much I loved the club.

It did not take me long to collect my gear from the office and one hour after the final whistle had signalled another victory for Wigan Athletic, I walked out of Springfield Park for the last time. The penny did not quite drop with the manager, because three days later he rang me at my shop in Manchester to tell me not to travel with the team to Aldershot that day. He did not even know that I had gone. I had obviously been sadly missed.

Extra-time

THIRTY-TWO

Swinging down the Lane

"THIS IS WHAT I CALL A FOOTBALL CLUB," I MUTTERED to Willie Donachie as we swept into the car park at Bramall Lane for our first day at Sheffield United.

Following the departure of Howard Kendall back to his first love, Everton, in the mid-1990s, the club had decided to upgrade player-coach Nigel Spackman to his first managerial role, and he had appointed Willie as his assistant and me as his chief scout.

Nigel and Willie are two of the nicest people in football. New coach Steve Thompson, who also started that day, isn't. That sounded like the perfect combination to me. 'Tommo' has been my pal for years, so I know him, I understand him and I love him. As players, the three of them have played almost 2,000 games between them, a tremendous amount of valuable experience to draw upon when you are looking after a football team.

During their careers, the names 'Spackman' and 'Donachie' have appeared on team sheets alongside some of the game's greatest footballers. They have always performed at the very highest level: Nigel with Chelsea, Liverpool, QPR and Rangers, while Willie won 35 Scotland international caps as a full-back for Manchester City. Both were very cultured players in their day.

In contrast, the words 'cultured' and 'Tommo' have never before featured in the same sentence. For Lincoln City and Charlton he was a rough, tough centre-half, with the world's biggest thighs. He slugged it out, toe to toe with some of the game's meanest centre-forwards, and he has got the scars to prove it. He was brought up as a kid in Sheffield supporting 'The Blades', so his new coaching position was extra special to him. Like me, he was thrilled to be an important member of the backroom team at Bramall Lane.

The 6am start didn't bother me, neither did the daily drive over the Pennines, despite being constantly overtaken and cut up on dangerous bends. I had Mr Donachie to keep me company every day, so it was a pleasure to go into work. Ivy kept my office sparkling and fragrant, Peggy served my coffee and toast piping hot in the mornings and I could hear the lovely Claire typing away next door. What more could a man ask for?

I even enjoyed Tony Currie's morning ritual of assaulting the highly temperamental photocopying machine that was situated just outside my office door.

"Bloody machine," he would holler as he tried to boot some life into it with that same left foot that had entranced the Blades faithful for so many years. Defeated, he would limp away in search of a cup of tea ...

"Peggy!"

Brilliant, I'd only been there five minutes and I felt completely at home. As the opening game of the season drew closer, I could sense that Nigel and Willie had put together a team good enough to really make an impact on this First Division, despite the fact that there were a number of other clubs with class players hoping to do the same, like Sunderland with Quinn and Phillips, and Middlesbrough with Merson and Gascoigne.

My job was to revamp the scouting system and recommend and help the manager to sign good players. Paul McGrath was the first. The club had already enticed Brian Deane back to Bramall Lane to play up front and it was felt that we needed somebody of equal strength and experience at the heart of the defence, alongside skipper Dave Holdsworth.

If we could find somebody like that, with either Alan Kelly or Simon Tracey in goal, it would give the team a very strong spine. They didn't come with more strength and experience than Paul McGrath, recently released by Derby County. One quick phone call set up a meeting at a hotel in Hale.

"Write down on the back of this menu what you want in wages."

And so we signed one of Britain's best-ever defenders in about 12 minutes flat. No messing, no agents, no haggling and no nonsense. That was how a great player with 83 international caps conducted his own transfer and he was magnificent both on and off the field in the short time he was a Sheffield United player.

I didn't want to change anything on the scouting side just for the sake of it. I wanted to give everybody a chance. I needed to meet and talk to the existing scouts, hear their views about various players, good and bad, and if their opinions generally coincided with mine then that would be great, it would mean that we could all be recommending the same quality of player to the manager.

A chance to do just that presented itself a little bit quicker than I expected when Nigel received a directive from the board to sell one of his two top-class goalkeepers. Most clubs in this division operate with a recognised number one and his understudy, but we were blessed with two number ones, Kelly and Tracey, each capable of holding down the top job at almost any other club in the league. They were both earning top wages, both felt that they should be in the team and there was little to choose between them, so the club decided to sell whichever of the two attracted the best offer.

I knew that the moment one of them was sold, Nigel would be in to see me expecting an immediate replacement. To be ready for this, I decided to invite my new team of scouts down to the ground individually to discuss the merits of various other goalkeepers. I had already mentally drawn up my own list of possible replacements as I welcomed scout number one into my office and settled him down with a cup of tea and a couple of slices of Peggy's finest. After a little preamble I asked him what he thought of Ade Bankole, the giant, young black goalkeeper who was beginning to make a name for himself at Crewe Alexandra.

"Yes, I've seen a lot of him," came the confident reply.

I was impressed.

"When he is good, he is brilliant, but when he is bad, he's bloody awful."

The pause while I waited for him to expound a little, to maybe explain his good and bad points, became embarrassing, but because he was a total stranger to me, I gave him the benefit of the doubt and then tried to make the uneasy silence a little more bearable by asking, possibly a bit hesitantly:

"Mmmm, is he erratic?"

"No, I think he's Nigerian."

This is going to be more difficult than I first thought.

"Thanks very much, close the door behind you on the way out."

THIRTY-THREE

Six Down, Four to Go

THE DRIVE OVER TO SHEFFIELD HAD BEEN WITHOUT
incident for a change. The beautiful early-morning sunshine
must have made the kamikaze drivers a little more tolerant of
each other. As usual, the eight o'clock news was just about to
start as Willie and I cruised into the deserted Tesco car park
in Abbeydale to meet Tommo.

Our early-morning ritual was a light breakfast and a chat
to sort out any prospective problems that might occur during
the day ahead, problems that we could sort out without
having to bother Nigel, leaving him free to concentrate solely
on the small matter of leading the club back into the
Premiership in nine months' time.

It was definitely the best part of the day, a croissant and a
cappuccino, just to get the brain in gear. Obviously there were
mornings when me and Tommo fancied 'The Magnificent 7',
Tesco's speciality of the house, a seven-piece fry-up for £2.99.
Unfortunately the joy of tucking into one of those beauties
just wasn't worth the disapproving look it would bring from
the super-fit, health-conscious Mr Donachie, so we always
abstained.

Anyway, this particular morning we were all too excited
to eat, because the following day the new season would be

kicking off and, try as we might, we just could not imagine another team in this division that had better players than we had, or a squad that had been better prepared.

We were to start our campaign against Sunderland on the Sunday. It was the day after everyone else because Sky Television had identified the two clubs involved as likely play-off candidates at the end of the season, and so had selected it as its televised game.

Shrewd judges those bosses at Sky, because that is exactly the way things turned out. But not one person in that victorious Blades dressing-room at full-time, after our superb 2–0 win, could possibly have foreseen the amazing chain of events that would take place between that first encounter with Sunderland on the opening day in August and the very last game of the season against them in the play-offs at the Stadium of Light in May.

During the summer break, the directors had been very accommodating. They had backed Nigel's request to strengthen an already strong squad by allowing him to bring in Vass Borbokis, a right wing-back from Greece. He made an immediate impact in that first game by scoring one goal and providing the cross for Jan Aage Fjortoft to score the other. Nicky Marker signed from Blackburn Rovers and with Paul McGrath from Derby County already added to the squad we had two very experienced defenders.

As the season got under way, strikers Marcelo and Traianos Dellas jetted in from Portugal and Greece respectively, while Bobby Ford made a somewhat shorter journey from Oxford. Every one of these players proved to be good signings, and in the case of 'Big Tri', it was the start of an adventure that would eventually earn him a Euro 2004 winner's medal with Greece in Portugal seven years later.

By far the biggest coup was the return of the prodigal son Brian Deane, whose appearance in that opening fixture produced shrieks of delight from the fans every time he touched the ball. He was costing a lot of money, but we all felt that he was worth it, such was his value to this particular club. The warmth and downright hysteria he generated among the supporters was quite amazing, and he immediately became their talisman.

It seemed as if everything just clicked into place from the very first kick of the new season, as the team embarked upon an opening sequence of 24 games that saw them lose just once, at West Brom.

Those 24 games had not been without their traumas, and during this period four key players, McGrath, Dane Whitehouse, Michael Vonk and David White, all suffered injuries so severe that none of them ever played for the club again. But once more the directors showed their commitment to the cause by allowing us to bring in Shaun Derry from Notts County, and the dressing-room was also livened up by the introduction of Graham Stuart from Everton and Dean Saunders from Nottingham Forest.

Stuart is a terrific professional, who willingly performs a variety of tasks for the team without ever complaining. A manager's dream, who was so unselfish that when presented with an open goal for Everton against Manchester United in the 1985 Cup final, instead of simply tapping the ball into the empty net for the 1–0 winner, chose instead to miss-hit it against the crossbar to enable Paul Rideout to knock in the rebound.

"I'm the only man ever to get a bobble at Wembley," he said whenever that miss was brought up in conversation. Which was as often as possible as far as Tommo and I were concerned.

Saunders was worth his transfer fee for his personality and influence in the dressing-room alone. There is nothing he hasn't achieved in the game. All the young players at the club looked up to him with his caps, his goals, his cup-winner's medals and his big transfer deals. He is an example of what can be achieved both career-wise and in terms of money if you work hard at your game, and to his credit Dean loved to play up to his own image.

"You're looking very chirpy this morning, Deano," I said, as he pulled up outside the ground in his gleaming, bright-red, top-of-the-range Mercedes. The apprentices were just getting off the bus at the time, each one admiring the car and dreaming.

"I'm made up," he replied. "I had a stroll around my garden last night and I found another lake."

Brilliant.

"Fred, I might be a bit late tomorrow morning. My car is in for a service, so I'll have to come by train."

"If you are late, Deano," I replied, "I'll be waiting at the door with a big bucket to collect your fine in."

"I'll give you a lift, Deano," volunteered Shaun Derry, who also lived in Nottingham.

"Great," said Saunders. "Come off the roundabout, turn

left, 100 yards, turn right, then a sharp left into my driveway, then you're about four miles from my house."

Priceless. I just hope that some of those kids from Bramall Lane will be saying the same things to youngsters in the game when they are the senior pros.

As we moved into December we were handily placed near the top of the league, and were fancied by most people as a certainty for promotion, if there is such a thing in football. Then, without warning, Everton manager Howard Kendall, having weighed up the players that he had inherited on his return to the club, came back to Bramall Lane and, in one fell swoop, signed our centre-half Carl Tiler, midfielder Mitch Ward and future Scottish international Don Hutchison in a triple transfer deal that certainly took 'The Tesco Three' by surprise, and I assume was also a shock to manager Nigel Spackman's system.

As Willie and I digested the news and our croissants with Tommo the next morning, we were all sensible enough to realise that there had to be a price to pay for all the players that we had signed. The books had to be balanced somehow, but we had not expected anything quite as drastic as this. We consoled ourselves with the thought that with three players suddenly gone on the same day, in addition to strikers Andy Scott and Andy Walker, and midfielder Mark Patterson who had also moved on, six players out would surely be enough.

We were galvanised by a rallying call from Tommo.

"Come on," he said defiantly, wiping the crumbs off his chops with the back of his hand. I really must explain to him what those napkins are for. "Let's get down to that training ground. We'll be all right. As long as we've got Nigel to lead us, as long as we've got Willie, the best coach in the country, and as long as we've got our talisman Brian and Jan Aage up front knocking in the goals, we will win this league."

THIRTY-FOUR

And Then There Were Two

"BRIAN DEANE'S A BIT LATE," SAID NIGEL, RUBBING his hands together at the prospect of fining our most prized asset a few bob. We all had a good chuckle, because we knew how painful it was for Brian whenever he was called upon to part with his cash. A fine, for him, was worse than a public flogging.

It was not like him to be late and as 11 o'clock approached our mood changed and we began to wonder if he was all right. I rang his mobile and found it to be switched off. It illustrated the seriousness of the situation because Brian's mobile phone appeared to be permanently welded to his ear.

Half an hour later he made contact with us.

"Where are you, Brian?"

"Just outside Lisbon."

"What are you doing in Gisburne?"

"No, Lisbon, Portugal."

"Oh right, I didn't know they had given you a few days off."

"I'm signing for Benfica."

"WHAT?"

It was mid-afternoon before Nigel got us all together in his office to try to make sense of this latest bombshell. Obviously it had been a financial decision by the board to sell him, but after pushing the boat out to bring Brian back, and the team doing so well, to release him after just six months at the club was disappointing to say the least.

"We'll be all right," said Tommo. "As long as we've still got Nigel to lead us, as long as we've still got Willie, the best coach in the country, and as long as we've still got Jan Aage to do Brian's job up front, we'll still get promotion."

"That was the other thing I have to tell you," said Nigel. "They've also sold Fjortoft, to Barnsley, today."

I rang Tommo from the car on our way home, once he'd had time to really digest this double whammy. He was remarkably upbeat under the circumstances.

"We'll be all right. As long as we've still got Nigel to lead us, as long as we've still got Willie, the best coach in the country, we'll still make those play-offs."

February started well for Sheffield United Football Club. FA Cup wins against Ipswich Town and Reading, and we were still sitting pretty near the top of the league. But the announcement that Joe Royle had been appointed as the new manager of Manchester City could only mean one thing. Willie would be joining him as his coach. They had been team-mates at Maine Road in the 1970s, they had rejuvenated Oldham Athletic together in the 1980s, and won the FA Cup together with Everton in the 1990s. It was inevitable.

"What do you think?" was Willie's first question the next morning as we set off for Sheffield. It was nice to be consulted, even though we both knew that the question was purely academic.

Tommo was gutted. Few people in this world command his total respect and Willie was one of those select few. As for me, it was like losing an arm as the 'Tesco Three' became two.

"We'll be all right," said Tommo, suddenly brightening up a bit as we made our way to the ground. "As long as we've got Nigel to lead us, we'll still be there or thereabouts."

Nigel's record as a manager so far had been first class. With 44 league and cup games played and only six defeats, it was promotion form. We had a vital sixth-round FA Cup tie coming up on Saturday away at Coventry City from the Premiership. It was the start of a very important week, and it seemed as though I had hardly been to sleep when I sat bolt upright in bed, jerked into life at 6.15am by the sound of the telephone ringing down my left ear-hole. It was Tommo.

"Nigel's gone."

I hadn't a clue what he was talking about. Gone on his holidays, gone down south to see his mum and dad, legs have gone, gone fishin'? What? But the local radio station in Sheffield had apparently just announced the shock resignation of manager Nigel Spackman.

The city of Sheffield was just stirring into life as I drove into Tesco's at ten minutes to eight, when Nigel himself rang me on my car phone to confirm the sad news.

"Morning, Dawn, two cappuccinos, two croissants and a large box of Anadin Extra, please."

"How are you going to get on now that you haven't got a manager?" she asked.

A fair question under the circumstances, and I looked at Tommo. He took a deep breath.

"We'll be all right. As long as we've still got, er, hmm, er, me and him. We'll finish in the top half of the table. No problem."

So, on Tuesday 3rd March 1998, Steven Paul Thompson achieved a lifetime's ambition when he was appointed as the manager (for one game only) of Sheffield United Football Club. I was delighted for him, but I just wished that the circumstances had been a little different. Of course, he asked me to be his assistant, possibly due to the fact that there were only the two of us left at the club, and we set about preparing a group of shell-shocked players for the game at Highfield Road on Saturday.

I think the general feeling among the directors was to install Tommo immediately, lose the Cup tie on Saturday and gain a few days' breathing space so that they could appoint a 'proper' manager before the next game.

We soon put a stop to that way of thinking by turning in a terrific performance against Coventry, with a goal from Marcelo earning us a well-deserved draw after Dion Dublin had put the home side in front from the penalty spot. We could have won it in the last second when substitute Petr Katchouro took advantage of an aberration by Coventry keeper Steve Ogrizovic and set off for goal almost from the halfway line with the giant, breathless keeper in hot pursuit. The ball was eventually scrambled clear for a corner.

Back in the dressing-room we were elated. Saunders and Stuart, who were both forced to miss the game, went round handing out praise and cups of tea in equal amounts, and as Tommo and I settled down together at the front of the coach for the journey home, it was announced on the radio that Steve Thompson was to be offered the manager's job until the end of the season.

"We'll have to get someone in to help us, pal," he said.

"Another week like this will just about finish us off."

I suggested that he bring back goalkeeping coach Jim Barron, formerly of Nottingham Forest, and the most handsome goalkeeper in the world. He had been unavailable for a few months, probably away making a film in Hollywood, and as well as being a good coach, he could always be relied upon to enhance any team photograph. That clinched it.

He joined us in time for the replay at Bramall Lane, which we won after extra-time and a penalty shoot-out, with young Wayne Quinn converting the vital one after Dion Dublin, David Burrows and Simon Howarth had all missed for Gordon Strachan's team. It was a night that all Blades fans will remember forever, just under 30,000 crammed into Bramall Lane. We had conceded a soft early goal and, despite being the better team, as the game wore on it just seemed that we were unlikely to score on this particular night, until, just before the end of normal time, skipper David Holdsworth forced in the equaliser.

As I moved among the players in the centre circle at the end of extra-time, just before the penalties, I knew in my heart that we would be the winners. We were destined to win that Cup tie; we would be in the semi-final of the FA Cup.

The games, though, were beginning to pile up and as the transfer deadline date drew near, we decided that we would approach the board with a view to beefing up our squad a little bit, to give our run in to the end of the season a boost.

The players that Tommo wanted to bring in were Paul Devlin from Birmingham City, Chris Wilder from Bradford City and Ian Hamilton from West Bromwich Albion, all for very reasonable fees. He had worked with Devlin and Wilder before so knew them both to be super pros, real assets to any dressing-room, and he had long admired Ian Hamilton's industrious midfield play. So we were delighted when we were told that all three players would love to come, and that the chairman had said that we could sign them on the proviso that we cleared it with the finance director first.

This was easier said than done, because he was away on tour in South Africa with Yorkshire County Cricket Club, and we were experiencing great difficulty in contacting him by telephone. As we arrived bright and early on Thursday, the actual transfer deadline day, we still hadn't been able to obtain his permission to sign the three players.

Terms had been formally agreed with the three clubs involved, and loosely with the players themselves, who were each sitting in their cars with the engines running in various parts of the country, awaiting a call from us to tell them to come and sign for Sheffield United.

Eventually we found him, told him the situation and he simply said:

"No, we can't afford them, we haven't got the money."

The news was relayed to the chairman.

"Of course we've got the money, ring him back and tell him."

Good news, we contacted South Africa to tell him.

"He doesn't know what he's talking about, we haven't got the money."

We rang the chairman.

"It's my money, ring back and just tell him that."

Great news, we rang South Africa again to inform him.

"Yes, I know it's his money, but I'm responsible for it. The answer is still no."

We rang the chairman yet again.

"Well, if he's so adamant, there is nothing more I can do."

"Okay, thanks, Chairman."

The afternoon dragged on, the five o'clock deadline loomed even larger.

"Why don't you give him one last ring?" I suggested with a sigh.

Tommo picked up the phone and dialled South Africa again.

"Hello, it's Tommo again, I was, er, well, me and Fred were thinking, well, me, really, I was just wondering if that's your final word on the subject. Basically, you know, what's the score?"

I could hear it loud and clear over the line, all the way from South Africa,

"Yes, Tommo, we are 83 for 3."

I'm sure that in far away South Africa he must have thought that Tommo had a hyena in the office with him, because I simply sat in the corner and howled and howled as Tommo gently replied:

"Oh good, how many has Vaughny got?"

I think that, possibly, he may well have been indulging himself in a little bit of fun at our expense throughout the day. Because a few minutes later he actually rang us back saying that he had found a few extra quid down the side of his chair that would enable us to sign the players we wanted.

We just had to hope that the three new faces would give us the impetus that we felt we needed. As long as they got to the ground before five o'clock in time to sign the forms.

THIRTY-FIVE

Shearer: Well It Would Be, Wouldn't It?

THE WEEK LEADING UP TO THE SEMI-FINAL WAS hectic and our preparations were not helped by a 3–0 defeat at Nottingham Forest the Wednesday before.

I honestly could not believe that I was just 90 minutes of football away from an FA Cup final at Wembley. It all seemed so pre-ordained; fate seemed to have taken a hand to give me one unlikely but glorious last finale—a little bit of recompense for all of those setbacks, heartache and being sick down that grid in Cromford Court. This was to be my belated reward for a lifetime of struggle in the game. Indeed, if Tommo was to be run over by a bus between now and the final, which could easily be arranged, I would actually be the one leading the team out at Wembley.

All we had to do was beat Newcastle United at Old Trafford. All we had to do was stop Alan Shearer from scoring; stop David Batty, John Barnes and Gary Speed from scheming; get past Stuart Pearce at the other end; and beat Shay Given in goal. If we could manage to do all of those things, then it would be the Twin Towers for us, and I could start deciding which bus driver I would approach to deal with Tommo.

But before then we had important league games to deal with, because it was vital to the club's future that we remained in the chase for promotion. Success in the play-offs could mean not just one but another Wembley appearance within ten days. Just like buses, you wait ages for one then two come along together. It was obviously meant to be.

It was a massive weekend for me. On Saturday I went along with my dad, just like the old days, to watch son Steven return to competitive football at Bamber Bridge after yet another major operation on his knee. This time he had been sidelined for a year, and it was a miracle to see him walk, let alone get a few crosses in, after what I had seen him suffer day after day.

After holding my breath for the whole 90 minutes, I was totally exhausted by the time I linked up with the Sheffield players at our hotel in Lymm for our big game the following day. A quick coffee with Tommo and match commentator Martyn Tyler was all I could manage before retiring to bed. It was the last game I ever went to with my dad; a memorable day indeed.

The atmosphere at Old Trafford was everything I hoped that a semi-final would be. As the coach drove us to the ground and we saw thousands of Sheffield United supporters waving and cheering, I really hoped that we could give them a win as a thank you for their tremendous support during what had been a turbulent season. Tommo was bursting with pride as a lifelong Blade. He was even pointing people out to me by name as we arrived at the players' entrance.

We just about squeezed past two surly, burly security guards on the door. Two more grudgingly grunted at us at the top of the tunnel, and I felt certain that I would have to show my passport to actually get into the dressing-room. I am sure that these lads could not have been the usual Manchester United security team, because I know quite a few of them very well, and they do their job with a little bit of charm to go with their efficiency.

After a quick walk on to the pitch with the players, a radio interview held me up for five minutes. I followed the players back up the tunnel towards the dressing-room on my own, only to be refused entry because I did not have the correct coloured piece of cardboard. Just what I needed, an argument guaranteed to trigger off a migraine on semi-final day, when I'm still working out how we are going to stop Shearer.

"I think it's in my coat, which is actually in the dressing-room," I said.

"It's no good in there," came the clever reply, and of course he was right.

I had encountered this sort of problem for about 40 years, but it was the last thing I needed that day. My embarrassment was only eased when Ian Rush, who had been with us on loan until a few days previously, but due to this fixture had returned to St James' Park, came striding towards me, blissfully unaware of the problem. He put his arm around my shoulder and walked me into my own dressing-room to wish his former team-mates good luck. I thought it was a nice gesture, and one that had just saved me the ignominy of having to wait outside the dressing-room door like the club mascot.

Tommo kept his team talk to the minimum; hopefully we had done enough talking leading up to the game. His pre-match talks had, I felt, been magnificent before every game—

motivational, inspirational, call them what you like but they were good. When he talked, the players listened, no back-chat, no smart-arsed answers, just sound football common sense.

Before one game, against Norwich at Bramall Lane, the lads were so gripped, or simply too frightened to interrupt him in full flow, that they all just sat and stared as water seeped under the bathroom door and lapped over his shoes and socks, threatening to flood the dressing-room. Young Jamie, one of the YT's, had left the bath running, and Tommo didn't even notice as he outlined his plans for the demolition of Norwich City. Today, after a few sharp reminders to certain players, he only needed three words to get the message across:

"Let's achieve immortality." And we were off.

As we took our seats on the bench, Tommo and I were embraced from behind by three pairs of arms. Don Hutchison, Carl Tiler and Mitch Ward, the three lads transferred to Everton earlier in the season, had come to wish us good luck. I will always think about that moment whenever I want to remember the good things about professional footballers.

Defensively, the game went according to plan in the first 45 minutes, but in truth we never really looked like scoring at the other end. Still, if somebody had offered me 0–0 at half-time before the game, I would have snatched their hand off. During the 15-minute break Tommo really went to work on his players, and I was completely focused on backing him up. So I was only faintly aware that the dressing-room door had opened and somebody had walked in.

"Who was that?" Jim Barron whispered in my ear.

I hadn't a clue; I hadn't even seen anybody walk through. Tommo was still motivating his players, exhorting just a little bit more from each one.

"Thar's reet, Tommo, you tell 'em."

The slight echo indicated that the voice was coming from the bathroom. A split second later, a drunken Sheffield United fan, decked out in a Blades scarf, huge rosette, red woolly hat, holding a matching dick in his hand, was surrounded by at least six of his heroes as he proceeded to piss down the front of his ripped jeans in shock.

He had somehow got past those surly, burly security guards. As he was physically ejected by our kitman Alan Gleason, I simply had to remark to the one who would not let me in, still diligently guarding the door like a sentry at Buckingham Palace:

"I suppose he had the right coloured ticket, did he?"

To which came the classic reply:

"He told me he was a director."

Ten minutes into the second half, a corner to them. No real problem, I thought. Holdsworth and Sandford had been dealing with them very well so far. Short one this time, though. I took a little more notice. To Stuart Pearce, who instead of swinging it into the box with his trusty left foot for Holdsworth and Sandford to head away again, simply played it back to John Barnes.

"Problem," I said to Tommo, digging him in the ribs with my elbow.

I just knew, some sixth sense told me. It was not really a dangerous position. Barnes was still fairly wide out on the left, but I knew. I could barely bring myself to look as he swung it in, right-footed, but now from a better angle. Shearer was the one who got there first. Well it would be, wouldn't it?

Alan Kelly made a terrific reflex save to knock the ball down on the line. It was Shearer who reacted first—well it would be, wouldn't it?—and hammered the ball high into the net from an inch. If Kelly had got his hand there at the same time, they would have found it in Stretford Precinct, three miles away.

The feeling that I had sitting on that bench at Old Trafford watching the game slip away was the same one that I had experienced many times before. It was just that this time the stakes were a lot higher. It was a feeling of hope rather than expectancy. Hope that the gods really were on my side; that we were going to get one really lucky bounce of the ball, because at 1–0 that is all it takes. But I knew in my heart that it was not going to happen.

After the final whistle I dragged myself round to everybody, shaking hands and telling really nice lads like Gary Speed that I hoped that they would go on to win it. I felt as though I was on auto-pilot as I trooped dejectedly up the tunnel, alone with my thoughts. All I could see in front of me was this giant black-and-white number nine, arms raised aloft, fists clenched in sheer delight. It was Alan Shearer—well it would be, wouldn't it?—all alone, savouring his great moment.

I slowed down to make sure that I did not catch up with him, and thought that if I, now aged 54 and never to get a sniff of a semi-final again, was ever to play against him in the future, he was definitely going to get the same treatment that I had dished out to Bobby Mitchell.

Our dressing-room was silent. Nobody moved. Nobody spoke. I'm not sure that anybody was even breathing. We were numb. I remember Alan Kelly just slumped on the floor. A luxury dressing-room and he preferred the floor. It was pointless trying to pick any of them up. Each one would have to come round in his own time, me included.

There was a knock on the dressing-room door. No one moved to open it, so Newcastle manager Kenny Dalglish popped his head in. Obviously he must have had the correct coloured ticket.

"Well played, lads. See you next season in the Premiership."

He then beat a hasty retreat.

"Not if you get fucking relegated," a voice replied.

We were beginning to pull ourselves together.

THIRTY-SIX

Virgin on the Ridiculous

I WOULD NOT HAVE THOUGHT IT POSSIBLE, BUT THE atmosphere at the Stadium of Light for the second leg of our play-off with Sunderland eclipsed even that great occasion at Old Trafford a month earlier. Since that disappointment, our form had been good, and we took a 2–1 lead from the home leg with us up to Wearside, hoping that it would be enough to see us through.

A disputed opening goal by Allan Johnston and the winner from Kevin Phillips, who rarely seemed to miss that season, condemned us to our second disappointment of missing out on Wembley within a month, and the journey back to Sheffield was the worst that I can remember.

The vital first goal was a particular sickener. We were all convinced from the bench that Bobby Ford had been clearly impeded before Johnston struck the crucial shot. It was scant consolation for us when, as we followed the last player out of the dressing-room for the second half, the referee took his life in his hands by saying:

"I've just seen it on TV, Tommo, and I made a mistake."

I had to admire his honesty, but that did not make me feel much better at two o'clock in the morning, travelling miserably down the A1 to oblivion.

In my opinion Steve Thompson had done a great job. He had inherited a football club fragmented by circumstances beyond his control, and by the sheer force of his personality had dragged it into the semi-finals of the FA Cup, and also into the play-offs. I felt that he had done more than enough to warrant the offer of the manager's job on a permanent basis as we both looked forward to a well-earned summer break.

That meant a limping holiday in Florida for me. The knee that had troubled me ever since that last game for Manchester City a mere 35 years previously was causing me considerable discomfort again. I was booked in for another operation in July, ironically on the very day that everyone else at Sheffield United would be reporting back to Bramall Lane for pre-season training.

The Virgin Atlantic flight had been first class, literally for us, as a result of having a daughter who has spent nearly all of her working life in the employment of Sir Richard Branson. She has been there so long that she must be due a testimonial. As senior flight attendant on our flight, she had ensured that the needs of her dear old mum and dad, with his dodgy knee, had been well and truly catered for. But even she could not make the baggage handlers move any quicker, and as we were waiting to nab our cases at Orlando Airport, the still athletic figure of John Deehan appeared by my side, accompanied by his wife.

John had been an accomplished striker during his playing career with Aston Villa, West Bromwich Albion and Norwich City, where he had become a particularly close friend of Steve Bruce prior to the centre-half's big move to Manchester United.

"What are you doing now?" he asked, keeping one eye out for his cases.

"Well, I am really chief scout at Sheffield United, but I finished the season as sort of assistant manager," I replied.

To be fair John Deehan handled it very well, but Mrs Deehan's face might just as well have been the back page of *The Sun*. A poker player she will never be, and as we eventually claimed our suitcases, I calmly informed Judith that Steve Bruce was to become the new manager of Sheffield United Football Club and that John Deehan would be his assistant. Not a word had been spoken, but I did not really need to buy a copy of the *Daily Mail* a week later to have it confirmed to me in black and white.

I had always got along very well with Steve Bruce and I admired him as a player. We had shared a few moments together here and there over the years, and I felt that if given the opportunity, I would enjoy working with him. I just hoped that he would keep Tommo on in a coaching capacity, as it was the very least he deserved.

I settled down to enjoy the rest of my holiday and tried to push the thought of the surgeon's scalpel to the back of my mind.

THIRTY-SEVEN

Kicked into Touch, One Last Time

SOMEWHERE IN MY SUBCONSCIOUS I COULD HEAR a voice.

"Would you like a cup of tea, Mr Eyre?"

Panic—I have never had a cup of tea in my life. The smell of it makes me want to vomit, and now here I was, while not in full possession of my faculties, almost being force-fed the horrible stuff. Nothing could have brought me to my senses any quicker, and I made a tentative grab for my right knee as soon as I realised where I was. The huge bandage confirmed that the operation had taken place at 6am and had hopefully been a success.

The doctors advised me to stay in hospital for at least 24 hours, but I didn't think they said it with much conviction so I took it as an invitation to go home, and Judith drove me back to Worsley shortly afterwards.

I was disappointed to miss Steve Bruce's first day in charge, but had told Tommo to let him know that I would be in the next day, because Judith had promised to drive me over to Sheffield.

I realised of course that this could prove to be a costly exercise, because while I caught up with things at Bramall

Lane, she intended to sample the delights of Meadowhall, the largest shopping mall in Europe. But I considered it to be a small price to pay for only having the one single day off work, when the recommended length of absence is three weeks.

It was five minutes past two as I hobbled in through our front door, and as if by radar the telephone began to ring.

"Hello, Fred, Steve Bruce here."

How nice. How thoughtful. Checking up on the welfare of a trusted member of staff. His first day in the job, too. He's going to make a great manager.

"Hello, Steve, sorry about today. Did Tommo tell you? I'll be in tomorrow, Judith's driving me over."

"Fred, I'll be bringing my own staff in, it's nothing per ... "

Zzzzzzzz. I could feel myself drifting off.

I hope it was the anaesthetic, but when you have been 'kicked into touch' as many times as I have, you never can tell.

THE GLORY GAME

The New Edition of the British Football Classic
HUNTER DAVIES

ISBN 1 84018 242 3
Available now
£7.99 (paperback)

When the first edition of *The Glory Game* was published in 1972, it was instantly hailed as the most accurate book about the life of a football team ever published. 'His accuracy is sufficiently uncanny to be embarrassing,' wrote Bob Wilson in the *New Statesman*. 'Brilliant, vicious, unmerciful,' wrote *The Sun*. It caused great controversy at the time. Hunter Davies was the first writer to be allowed into the inner sanctums of a top football team (Tottenham Hotspur), and his pen spared nothing and no one. Now the main controversies have been forgotten. Or forgiven. Instead, his work has turned into a classic, probably the best book about football ever written.

> '*The Glory Game* engages the mind while revealing the soul of the beautiful game.'
>
> *The Herald*

THE GAME

'66!

The Inside Story of England's 1966 World Cup Triumph
ROGER HUTCHINSON

ISBN 1 84018 603 8
Available now
£7.99 (paperback)

'. . . it is now!' With those legendary three words the 1966 World Cup final came to an end. England had won, and at 5.15 p.m., 30 July 1966, Bobby Moore wiped his hands on his shorts, shook hands with the Queen and took delivery of the Jules Rimet trophy before a worldwide television audience of 600 million. It was, and it remains, the single greatest British sporting achievement.

Roger Hutchinson's account of England's World Cup triumph sparkles with wit and with sporting brilliance. It is the story of a sporting adventure which, far from putting football back 100 years, as some detractors of Sir Alf Ramsey said at the time, catapulted it unwillingly into the future.

> 'Book of the Month . . . If you only read one book about the 1966 World Cup, make sure it's this one' *****
>
> *FourFourTwo*

FIELDS OF GLORY,
PATHS OF GOLD

The History of European Football
KEVIN CONNOLLY AND RAB MacWILLIAM

ISBN 1 84596 099 8
May 2006
£7.99 (paperback)

Fields of Glory, Paths of Gold tells the remarkable story of the growth of European football over the past 125 years.

Packed with intriguing stories and facts, it:

- charts the foundation and development of the club sides that shaped European football;
- assesses the great international teams that emerged over the years;
- highlights the exceptional players who revolutionised the game, from Johan Cruyff to Franz Beckenbauer;
- examines the important work of visionary managers, such as Herbert Chapman and Sir Alex Ferguson;
- traces the roots of the Champions League, showing how the competition was designed to favour the elite from western Europe's major leagues.

This authoritative and entertaining volume is a must-read for football fans of all ages.

> 'Meticulously charts the development of the European game'
>
> *Evenng Standard*

THE FASHION OF FOOTBALL

From Best to Beckham, From Mod to Label Slave

PAOLO HEWITT AND MARK BAXTER

ISBN 1 84596 050 5
Available now
£7.99 (paperback)

Fashion has played a major part in the elevation of footballers to iconic status in modern society. Whether it be George Best's famous clothes shops, Alan Hudson's haircut or David Beckham's unique dress sense, the worlds of fashion and football have often intertwined. This relationship is brilliantly brought to life in *The Fashion of Football*. The journey starts with the players and focuses on stars such as George Best, Bobby Moore, Steve Perryman, Alan Hudson, Mike Summerbee, Darren Ward and David Beckham, as well as a wider range of famous names, like the tailor Dougie Hayward, who designed Bobby Moore's suits. The book then moves on to chart the many influential street fashions that have emanated from the terraces over the years.

This is a unique and riveting read, brought to life by photographs taken by the great Terry O'Neill, one of the first lensmen to spot and celebrate this remarkable relationship.

'A bible for the fashion-conscious football fan'
The Times

'A unique and interesting guide to the trends followed by, and in some cases set by, footballers and fans over the last 40 years' ****

FourFourTwo

THE GAFFTA AWARDS

LARRY RYAN

ISBN 1 84018 922 3
Available now
£6.99 (paperback)

The Gaffta Awards is a book about football's most enduring characters. You know who we mean – the game's talking heads, the selfless men who entertain us as royally from behind the microphone as their more athletic comrades do on the pitch. Despite all the media attention football receives, no one has seen fit to devise an awards system for the verbal geniuses of the modern game. Until now.

This is the definitive study of 'guff', our umbrella term for all the gaffes, faux pas and general foolishness so prevalent in football today. Thrill as Uncle Bobby Robson, King Kev and Gordon Strachan battle it out for the Best Gaffer gong. In the Best Commentator category, sheepskin statto Motty challenges for glory against big-hitters Clive Tyldesley (Manchester United's number-one fan) and the sadly departed Brian Moore. Despite his fall from grace, Big Ron's sterling work developing Ronglish – the official language of the commentary box – sees him in with a real chance. That said, excitable newcomer Chris Kamara will shout him down all the way to the awards podium.

> 'Highly amusing'
> *The Times*

> 'Hilarious'
> *Daily Star*

BALLS

Tales from Football's Nether Regions
PAUL BROWN

ISBN 1 84596 063 7
Available now
£7.99 (paperback)

Balls is an eclectic collection of amazing true stories from the world of football, revealing the bizarre and hilarious reality behind the beautiful game.

- What possessed a World Cup superstar to kidnap 120 Cameroonian pygmies?
- Which ex-goalkeeper genuinely believes he is the Son of God?
- Why was a former Southampton full-back offered the throne of Albania?
- Was a former Everton striker really hung for stealing a sheep in Australia?
- And whatever happened to Maradona's fake rubber penis?

Balls is an unashamed celebration of the mad, bad and stupid aspects of football – the greatest game in the world.

'The best of the bunch' – Sports Books of the Year
The Independent

'Football has been given compendiums of curiosities before, but surely none so comprehensive, so remorseless as this . . . every page teems with anecdotes' ****
FourFourTwo